EUREKA MATH™

A Story of Ratios

Grade 8, Module 5
Examples of Functions from Geometry

A Wiley Brand

When do you know you really understand something? One test is to see if you can explain it to someone else—well enough that *they* understand it. Eureka Math routinely requires students to "turn and talk" and explain the math they learned to their peers.

That is because the goal of Eureka Math (which you may know as the EngageNY math modules) is to produce students who are not merely literate, but fluent, in mathematics. By fluent, we mean not just knowing what process to use when solving a problem but understanding why that process works.

Here's an example. A student who is fluent in mathematics can do far more than just name, recite, and apply the Pythagorean theorem to problems. She can explain why $a^2 + b^2 = c^2$ is true. She not only knows the theorem can be used to find the length of a right triangle's hypotenuse, but can apply it more broadly—such as to find the distance between any two points in the coordinate plane, for example. She also can see the theorem as the glue joining seemingly disparate ideas including equations of circles, trigonometry, and vectors.

By contrast, the student who has merely memorized the Pythagorean theorem does not know why it works and can do little more than just solve right triangle problems by rote. The theorem is an abstraction—not a piece of knowledge, but just a process to use in the limited ways that she has been directed. For her, studying mathematics is a chore, a mere memorizing of disconnected processes.

Eureka Math provides much more. It offers students math knowledge that will serve them well beyond any test. This fundamental knowledge not only makes wise citizens and competent consumers, but it gives birth to budding physicists and engineers. Knowing math deeply opens vistas of opportunity.

A student becomes fluent in math—as they do in any other subject—by following a course of study that builds their knowledge of the subject, logically and thoroughly. In Eureka Math, concepts flow logically from PreKindergarten through high school. The "chapters" in the story of mathematics are "A Story of Units" for the elementary grades, followed by "A Story of Ratios" in middle school and "A Story of Functions" in high school.

This sequencing is joined with a mix of new and old methods of instruction that are proven to work. For example, we utilize an exercise called a "sprint" to develop students' fluency with standard algorithms (routines for adding, subtracting, multiplying, and dividing whole numbers and fractions). We employ many familiar models and tools such as the number line and tape diagrams (aka bar diagrams). A newer model highlighted in the curriculum is the number bond (illustrated below), which clearly shows how numbers are comprised of other numbers.

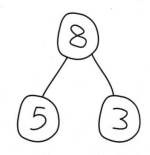

Eureka Math is designed to help accommodate different types of classrooms and serve as a resource for educators, who make decisions based on the needs of students. The "vignettes" of teacher-student interactions included in the curriculum are not scripts, but exemplars illustrating methods of instruction recommended by the teachers who have crafted our curricula.

Eureka Math has been adopted by districts from East Meadows, NY to Lafayette, LA to Chula Vista, CA. At Eureka Math we are excited to have created the most transparent math curriculum in history—every lesson, all classwork, and every problem is available online.

Many of us have less than joyful memories of learning mathematics: lots of memorization, lots of rules to follow without understanding, and problems that didn't make any sense. What if a curriculum came along that gave children a chance to avoid that math anxiety and replaced it with authentic understanding, excitement, and curiosity? Like a NY educator attending one of our trainings said: "Why didn't I learn mathematics this way when I was a kid? It is so much easier than the way I learned it!"

Eureka!

Lynne Munson
Washington DC
September 2014

Mathematics Curriculum

Table of Contents[1]

Examples of Functions from Geometry

Topics A–B (assessment 1 day, return 1 day, remediation or further applications 2 days)

---

[1] Each lesson is ONE day and ONE day is considered a 45-minute period.

Grade 8 • Module 5

Examples of Functions from Geometry

OVERVIEW

In Topic A of Module 5, students learn the concept of a function and why functions are necessary for describing geometric concepts and occurrences in everyday life. The module begins by explaining the important role functions play in making predictions. For example, if an object is dropped, a function allows us to determine its height at a specific time. To this point, our work has relied on assumptions of constant rates; here, students are given data that shows that objects do not always travel at a constant speed. Once we explain the concept of a function, we then provide a formal definition of function. A function is defined as an assignment to each input, exactly one output (**8.F.A.1**). Students learn that the assignment of some functions can be described by a mathematical rule or formula. With the concept and definition firmly in place, students begin to work with functions in real-world contexts. For example, students relate constant speed and other proportional relationships (**8.EE.B.5**) to linear functions. Next, students consider functions of discrete and continuous rates and understand the difference between the two. For example, we ask students to explain why they can write a cost function for a book, but they cannot input 2.6 into the function and get an accurate cost as the output.

Students apply their knowledge of linear equations and their graphs from Module 4 (**8.EE.B.5**, **8.EE.B.6**) to graphs of linear functions. Students know that the definition of a graph of a function is the set of ordered pairs consisting of an input and the corresponding output (**8.F.A.1**). Students relate a function to an input-output machine: a number or piece of data, goes into the machine, known as the input, and a number or piece of data comes out of the machine, known as the output. In Module 4, students learned that a linear equation graphs as a line and that all lines are graphs of linear equations. In Module 5, students inspect the rate of change of linear functions and conclude that the rate of change is the slope of the graph of a line. They learn to interpret the equation $y = mx + b$ (**8.EE.B.6**) as defining a linear function whose graph is a line (**8.F.A.3**). Students will also gain some experience with non-linear functions, specifically by compiling and graphing a set of ordered pairs, and then by identifying the graph as something other than a straight line.

Once students understand the graph of a function, they begin comparing two functions represented in different ways (**8.EE.C.8**), similar to comparing proportional relationships in Module 4. For example, students are presented with the graph of a function and a table of values that represent a function, and are then asked to determine which function has the greater rate of change (**8.F.A.2**). Students are also presented with functions in the form of an algebraic equation or written description. In each case, students examine the average rate of change and know that the one with the greater rate of change must overtake the other at some point.

In Topic B, students apply their knowledge of volume from previous grade levels (**5.MD.C.3**, **5.MD.C.5**) to the learning of the volume formulas for cones, cylinders, and spheres (**8.G.C.9**). First, students are reminded of what they already know about volume, that volume is always a positive number that describes the hollowed out portion of a solid figure that can be filled with water. Next, students use what they learned about the area of circles (**7.G.B.4**) to determine the volume formulas of cones and cylinders. In each case, physical models will be used to explain the formulas, first with a cylinder seen as a stack of circular disks that provide the height of the cylinder. Students consider the total area of the disks in three dimensions understanding it as volume of a cylinder. Next, students make predictions about the volume of a cone that has the same dimensions as a cylinder. A demonstration shows students that the volume of a cone is one-third the volume of a cylinder with the same dimension, a fact that will be proved in Module 7. Next, students compare the volume of a sphere to its circumscribing cylinder (i.e., the cylinder of dimensions that touches the sphere at points, but does not cut off any part of it). Students learn that the formula for the volume of a sphere is two-thirds the volume of the cylinder that fits tightly around it. Students extend what they learned in Grade 7 (**7.G.B.6**) about how to solve real-world and mathematical problems related to volume from simple solids to include problems that require the formulas for cones, cylinders, and spheres.

Focus Standards

Define, evaluate, and compare functions.

8.F.A.1   Understand that a function is a rule that assigns to each input exactly one output. The graph of a function is the set of ordered pairs consisting of an input and the corresponding output.[2]

8.F.A.2   Compare properties of two functions each represented in a different way (algebraically, graphically, numerically in tables, or by verbal descriptions). *For example, given a linear function represented by a table of values and a linear function represented by an algebraic expression, determine which function has the greater rate of change.*

8.F.A.3   Interpret the equation $y = mx + b$ as defining a linear function whose graph is a straight line; give examples of functions that are not linear. *For example, the function $A = s^2$ giving the area of a square as a function of its side length is not linear because its graph contains the points $(1, 1)$, $(2, 4)$ and $(3, 9)$ which are not on a straight line.*

Solve real-world and mathematical problems involving volume of cylinders, cones, and spheres.

8.G.C.9   Know the formulas for the volumes of cones, cylinders, and spheres and use them to solve real-world and mathematical problems.

---

[2] Function notation is not required in Grade 8.

Foundational Standard

Geometric measurement: Understand concepts of volume and relate volume to multiplication and to addition.

5.MD.C.3 Recognize volume as an attribute of solid figures and understand concepts of volume measurement.

    a. A cube with side length 1 unit, called a "unit cube," is said to have "one cubic unit" of volume, and can be used to measure volume.

    b. A solid figure which can be packed without gaps or overlaps using n unit cubes is said to have a volume of n cubic units.

5.MD.C.5 Relate volume to the operations of multiplication and addition, and solve real-world and mathematical problems involving volume.

    a. Find the volume of a right rectangular prism with whole-number side lengths by packing it with unit cubes, and show that the volume is the same as would be found by multiplying the edge lengths, equivalently by multiplying the height by the area of the base. Represent threefold whole-number products as volumes, e.g., to represent the associative property of multiplication.

    b. Apply the formulas $V = l \times w \times h$ and $V = b \times h$ for rectangular prisms to find volumes of right rectangular prisms with whole number edge lengths in the context of solving real world and mathematical problems.

    c. Recognize volume as additive. Find volume of solid figures composed of two non-overlapping right rectangular prisms by adding the volumes of the non-overlapping parts, applying this technique to real world problems.

Solve real-life and mathematical problems involving angle measure, area, surface area, and volume.

7.G.B.4 Know the formulas for the area and circumference of a circle and use them to solve problems; give an informal derivation of the relationship between the circumference and area of a circle.

7.G.B.6 Solve real-world and mathematical problems involving area, volume, and surface area of two- and three-dimensional objects composed of triangles, quadrilaterals, polygons, cubes, and right prisms.

Understand the connections between proportional relationships, lines, and linear equations.

8.EE.B.5 Graph proportional relationships, interpreting the unit rate as the slope of the graph. Compare two different proportional relationships represented in different ways. *For example, compare a distance-time graph to a distance-time equation to determine which of two moving objects has greater speed.*

8.EE.B.6   Use similar triangles to explain why the slope m is the same between any two distinct points on a non-vertical line in the coordinate plane; derive the equation $y = mx$ for a line through the origin and the equation $y = mx + b$ for a line intercepting the vertical axis at b.

Analyze and solve linear equations and pairs of simultaneous linear equations.

8.EE.C.7   Solve linear equations in one variable.

     a.   Give examples of linear equations in one variable with one solution, infinitely many solutions, or no solutions. Show which of these possibilities is the case by successively transforming the given equation into simpler forms, until an equivalent equation of the form $x = a$, $a = a$, or $a = b$ results (where a and b are different numbers).

     b.   Solve linear equations with rational number coefficients, including equations whose solutions require expanding expressions using the distributive property and collecting like terms.

8.EE.C.8   Analyze and solve pairs of simultaneous linear equations.

     a.   Understand that solutions to a system of two linear equations in two variables correspond to points of intersection of their graphs, because points of intersection satisfy both equations simultaneously.

     b.   Solve systems of two linear equations in two variables algebraically, and estimate solutions by graphing the equations. Solve simple cases by inspection. *For example, $3x + 2y = 5$ and $3x + 2y = 6$ have no solution because $3x + 2y$ cannot simultaneously be 5 and 6.*

     c.   Solve real-world and mathematical problems leading to two linear equations in two variables. *For example, given coordinates for two pairs of points, determine whether the line through the first pair of points intersects the line through the second pair.*

Focus Standards for Mathematical Practice

MP.2   **Reason abstractly or quantitatively**. Students examine, interpret, and represent functions symbolically. They make sense of quantities and their relationships in problem situations. For example, students make sense of values as they relate to the total cost of items purchased or a phone bill based on usage in a particular time interval. Students use what they know about rate of change to distinguish between linear and non-linear functions. Further, students contextualize information gained from the comparison of two functions.

MP.6   **Attend to precision**. Students use notation related to functions in general, as well as volume formulas. Students are expected to clearly state the meaning of the symbols used in order to communicate effectively and precisely to others. Students attend to precision when they interpret data generated by functions. They know when claims are false; for example, calculating the height of an object after it falls for -2 seconds. Students also understand that a table of values is an incomplete *representation* of a continuous function, as an infinite number of values can be found for a function.

MP.8   **Look for and express regularity in repeated reasoning.** Students will use repeated computations to determine equations from graphs or tables. While focused on the details of a specific pair of numbers related to the input and output of a function, students will maintain oversight of the process. As students develop equations from graphs or tables, they will evaluate the reasonableness of their equation as they ensure that the desired output is a function of the given input.

Terminology

New or Recently Introduced Terms

- **Function** (A *function* is a rule that assigns to each input exactly one output.)
- **Input** (The number or piece of data that is put into a function is the *input*.)
- **Output** (The number or piece of data that is the result of an input of a function is the *output*.)

Familiar Terms and Symbols[3]

- Volume
- Area
- Solids
- Linear equation
- Non-linear equation
- Rate of change

Suggested Tools and Representations

- 3D solids: cones, cylinders, and spheres.

Assessment Summary

Assessment Type	Administered	Format	Standards Addressed
End-of-Module Assessment Task	After Topic B	Constructed response with rubric	8.F.A.1, 8.F.A.2, 8.F.A.3, 8.G.C.9

---

[3] These are terms and symbols students have seen previously.

Module 5:   Examples of Functions from Geometry

8
GRADE

Mathematics Curriculum

Topic A:

Functions

8.F.A.1, 8.F.A.2, 8.F.A.3

Focus Standard:	8.F.A.1	Understand that a function is a rule that assigns to each input exactly one output. The graph of a function is the set of ordered pairs consisting of an input and the corresponding output.
	8.F.A.2	Compare properties of two functions each represented in a different way (algebraically, graphically, numerically in tables, or by verbal descriptions). *For example, given a linear function represented by a table of values and a linear function represented by an algebraic expression, determine which function has the greater rate of change.*
	8.F.A.3	Interpret the equation $y = mx + b$ as defining a linear function, whose graph is a straight line; give examples of functions that are not linear. *For example, the function $A = s^2$ giving the area of a square as a function of its side length is not linear because its graph contains the points $(1, 1)$, $(2, 4)$ and $(3, 9)$, which are not on a straight line.*
Instructional Days:	8	
	Lesson 1:	The Concept of a Function (P)[1]
	Lesson 2:	Formal Definition of a Function (S)
	Lesson 3:	Linear Functions and Proportionality (P)
	Lesson 4:	More Examples of Functions (P)
	Lesson 5:	Graphs of Functions and Equations (E)
	Lesson 6:	Graphs of Linear Functions and Rate of Change (S)
	Lesson 7:	Comparing Linear Functions and Graphs (E)
	Lesson 8:	Graphs of Simple Non-Linear Functions (E)

---

[1] Lesson Structure Key: **P**-Problem Set Lesson, **M**-Modeling Cycle Lesson, **E**-Exploration Lesson, **S**-Socratic Lesson

Lesson 1 relies on students' understanding of constant rate, a skill developed in previous grade levels and reviewed in Module 4 (**6.RP.A.3b**, **7.RP.A.2**). Students are confronted with the fact that the concept of constant rate, which requires the assumption that a moving object travels at a constant speed, cannot be applied to all moving objects. Students examine a graph and a table that demonstrates the non-linear effect of gravity on a falling object. This example provides the reasoning for the need of functions. In Lesson 2, students continue their investigation of time and distance data for a falling object and learn that the scenario can be expressed by a formula. Students are introduced to the terms input and output and learn that a function assigns to each input exactly one output. Though students will not learn the traditional "vertical-line test," students will know that the graph of a function is the set of ordered pairs consisting of an input and the corresponding output. Students also learn that not all functions can be expressed by a formula, but when they are, the function rule allows us to make predictions about the world around us. For example, with respect to the falling object, the function allows us to predict the height of the object for any given time interval.

In Lesson 3, constant rate is revisited as it applies to the concept of linear functions and proportionality in general. Lesson 4 introduces students to the fact that not all rates are continuous. That is, we can write a cost function for the cost of a book, yet we cannot realistically find the cost of 3.6 books. Students are also introduced to functions that do not use numbers at all, as in a function where the input is a card from a standard deck and the output is the suit.

Lesson 5 is when students begin graphing functions of two variables. Students graph linear and non-linear functions and the guiding question of the lesson, "Why not just look at graphs of equations in two variables?", is answered because not all graphs of equations are graphs of functions. Students continue their work on graphs of linear functions in Lesson 6. In this lesson, students investigate the rate of change of functions and conclude that the rate of change for linear functions is the slope of the graph. In other words, this lesson solidifies the fact that the equation $y = mx + b$ defines a linear function, whose graph is a straight line.

With the knowledge that the graph of a linear function is a straight line, students begin to compare properties of two functions that are expressed in different ways in Lesson 7. One example of this relates to comparison of phone plans. Students are provided a graph of a function for one plan and an equation of a function that represents another plan. In other situations, students will be presented with functions that are expressed algebraically, graphically, and numerically in tables or are described verbally. Students must use the information provided to answer questions about the rate of change of each function. In Lesson 8, students work with simple non-linear functions of area and volume and their graphs.

Lesson 1: The Concept of a Function

Student Outcomes

- Students know that a function allows us to make predictions about the distance an object moves in any time interval. Students calculate average speed of a moving object over specific time intervals.
- Students know that constant rate cannot be assumed for every situation and use proportions to analyze the reasoning involved.

Lesson Notes

In this and subsequent lessons the data would ideally be gathered live using technology, making the data more real for students and creating an interactive element for the lessons. Time and resources permitting, consider gathering live data to represent the functions in this module.

Much of the discussion in this module is based on parts from the following sources:

H. Wu, Introduction to School Algebra, http://math.berkeley.edu/~wu/Algebrasummary.pdf

H. Wu, Teaching Geometry in Grade 8 and High School According to the Common Core Standards
http://math.berkeley.edu/~wu/CCSS-Geometry.pdf

Classwork

Discussion (4 minutes)

- We have been studying numbers, and we seem to be able to do all the things we want to with numbers, so why do we need to learn about functions? The answer is that if we expand our vision and try to find out about things that we *ought to know*, then we discover that numbers are not enough. We experienced some of this when we wrote linear equations to describe a situation. For example, average speed and constant rate allowed us to write two variable linear equations that could then be used to predict the distance an object would travel for any desired length of time.
- Functions also allow us to make predictions. In some cases, functions simply allow us to classify the data in our environment. For example, a function might state a person's age or gender. In these examples, a linear equation is unnecessary.
- In the last module we focused on situations where the rate of change was always constant. That is, each situation could be expressed as a linear equation. However, there are many occasions for which the rate is not constant. Therefore, we must attend to each situation to determine whether or not the rate of change is constant and can be modeled with a linear equation.

 | Lesson 1:   The Concept of a Function

9

Example 1 (7 minutes)

This example is used to point out that in much of our previous work, we assumed a constant rate. This is in contrast to the next example, where constant rate cannot be assumed. Encourage students to make sense of the problem and attempt to solve it on their own. The goal is for students to develop a sense of what predicting means in this context.

MP.1

Example 1

Suppose a moving object travels 256 feet in 4 seconds. Assume that the object travels at a constant speed, that is, the motion of the object is linear with a constant rate of change. Write a linear equation in two variables to represent the situation, and use it to make predictions about the distance traveled over various intervals of time.

Number of seconds (x)	Distance traveled in feet (y)
1	64
2	128
3	192
4	256

- Suppose a moving object travels 256 feet in 4 seconds. Assume that the object travels at a constant speed, that is, the motion of the object is linear with a constant rate of change. Write a linear equation in two variables to represent the situation, and use it to make predictions about the distance traveled over various intervals of time.

  □ *Let y represent the distance traveled and x represent the time it takes to travel y feet.*

$$\frac{256}{4} = \frac{y}{x}$$

$$y = \frac{256}{4}x$$

$$y = 64x$$

- What are some of the predictions that this equation allows us to make?

  □ *After one second, or when $x = 1$, the distance traveled is 64 feet.*

Accept any reasonable predictions that the students make.

- Use your equation to complete the table.
- What is the average speed of the moving object from zero to three seconds?

  □ *The average speed is 64 feet per second. We know that the object has a constant rate of change; therefore, we expect the average speed to be the same over any time interval.*

Example 2 (15 minutes)

- We have already made predictions about the location of a moving object. Now, here is some more information. The object is a stone, being dropped from a height of 256 feet. It takes exactly 4 seconds for the stone to hit the ground. How far does the stone drop in the first 3 seconds? What about the last 3 seconds? Can we assume constant speed in this situation? That is, can this situation be expressed using a linear equation?

Lesson 1:   The Concept of a Function

Example 2

The object, a stone, is dropped from a height of 256 feet. It takes exactly 4 seconds for the stone to hit the ground. How far does the stone drop in the first 3 seconds? What about the last 3 seconds? Can we assume constant speed in this situation? That is, can this situation be expressed using a linear equation?

Number of seconds (x)	Distance traveled in feet (y)
1	16
2	64
3	144
4	256

Provide students time to discuss this in pairs. Lead a discussion where students share their thoughts with the class. It is likely that they will say this is a situation that can be modeled with a linear equation, just like the moving object in Example 1. Continue with the discussion below.

- If this is a linear situation, then from the table we developed in Example 1 we already know the stone will drop 192 feet in any 3 second interval. That is, the stone drops 192 feet in the first 3 seconds and in the last 3 seconds.

To provide a visual aid, consider viewing the 10 second "ball drop" video at the following link: http://www.youtube.com/watch?v=KrX_zLuwOvc. You may need to show it more than once.

- If we were to slow the video down and record the distance the ball dropped after each second, we would collect the following data:

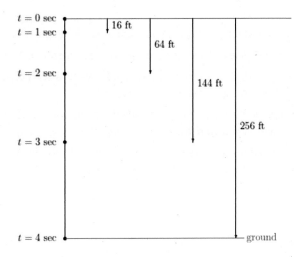

- Choose a prediction that was made about the distance traveled before we learned more about the situation. Was it accurate? How do you know?

Students should realize that the predictions were not accurate for this situation. Guide their thinking using the discussion points below.

- According to the data, how many feet did the stone drop in 3 seconds?
  - *The stone dropped 144 feet.*

- How can that be? It must be that our initial assumption of constant rate was incorrect. Let's organize the information from the diagram above in a table:

  What predictions can we make now?

  - *After one second, $x = 1$, the stone dropped 16 feet, etc.*

- Let's make a prediction based on a value of x that is not listed in the table. How far did the stone drop in the first 3.5 seconds? What have we done in the past to figure something like this out?

  - *We wrote a proportion using the known times and distances.*

Allow students time to work with their proportions. Encourage them to use more than one set of data to determine an answer.

  - *Sample student work:*

    Let x be the distance the stone drops.

$$\frac{16}{1} = \frac{x}{3.5} \qquad\qquad \frac{64}{2} = \frac{x}{3.5} \qquad\qquad \frac{144}{3} = \frac{x}{3.5}$$
$$x = 56 \qquad\qquad\quad 2x = 224 \qquad\qquad\quad 3x = 504$$
$$\qquad\qquad\qquad x = 112 \qquad\qquad\quad x = 168$$

- Is it reasonable that the stone would drop 56 feet in 3 seconds? Explain.

  - *No, it is not reasonable. Our data shows that after 2 seconds the stone has already dropped 64 feet. Therefore, it is impossible that it could have only dropped 56 feet in 3.5 seconds.*

- What about 112 feet in 3.5 seconds. How reasonable is that answer? Explain.

  - *The answer of 112 feet in 3.5 seconds is not reasonable either. The data shows that the stone dropped 144 feet in 3 seconds.*

- What about 168 feet in 3.5 seconds. What do you think about that answer? Explain.

  - *That answer is the most likely because at least it is greater than the recorded 144 feet in 3 seconds.*

- What makes you think that the work done with a third proportion will give us a correct answer when the first two did not? Can we rely on this method for determining an answer?

  - *This does not seem to be a reliable method. If we had only done one computation and not evaluated the reasonableness of our answer, we would have been wrong.*

- What this means is that the table we used does not tell the whole story about the falling stone. If we looked at more intervals of time, say every half second, we would have the following table:

Number of seconds (x)	Distance traveled in feet (y)
0.5	4
1	16
1.5	36
2	64
2.5	100
3	144
3.5	196
4	256

Lesson 1:   The Concept of a Function

- Choose a prediction you made before this table. Was it accurate? Why might one want to be able to predict?

Students will likely have made predictions that were not accurate. Have a discussion with students about why we want to make predictions at all. They should recognize that making predictions helps us make sense of the world around us. Consider any scientific discovery. It began with a prediction, then an experiment to prove or disprove the prediction, followed by some conclusion.

- Now it is clear that none of our answers for the distance traveled in 3.5 seconds were correct. In fact, the stone dropped 196 feet in the first 3.5 seconds. Does the above table capture the motion of the stone? Explain?

  □ *No. There are intervals of time between those in the table. For example, the distance it drops in 1.6 seconds is not represented.*

- If we were to record the data for every 0.1 seconds that pass, would that be enough to capture the motion of the stone?

  □ *No. There would still be intervals of time not represented. For example, 1.61 seconds.*

- In fact, we would have to calculate to an infinite number of decimals to tell the whole story about the falling stone. To tell the whole story, we would need information about where the stone is after the first t seconds for *every* t satisfying $0 \leq t \leq 4$.

- This kind of information is more than just a few numbers. It is about all of the distances (in feet) the stone drops in t seconds from a height of 256 feet for all t satisfying $0 \leq t \leq 4$.

- The inequality, $0 \leq t \leq 4$, helps us tell the whole story about the falling stone. The infinite collection of distances associated with every t in $0 \leq t \leq 4$ is an example of a function. Only a function can tell the whole story because functions allow us to predict with accuracy.

Exercises 1–6 (10 minutes)

Students complete Exercises 1–6 in pairs or small groups.

Exercises 1–6

Use the table to answer Exercises 1–5.

Number of seconds (x)	Distance traveled in feet (y)
0.5	4
1	16
1.5	36
2	64
2.5	100
3	144
3.5	196
4	256

1. Name two predictions you can make from this table.

   Sample student responses:

   After 2 seconds, the object traveled 64 feet. After 3.5 seconds, the object traveled 196 feet.

| Lesson 1: | The Concept of a Function |

2. Name a prediction that would require more information.

Sample student response:

We would need more information to predict the distance traveled after 3.75 seconds.

3. What is the average speed of the object between zero and three seconds? How does this compare to the average speed calculated over the same interval in Example 1?

$$Average\ Speed = \frac{distance\ traveled\ over\ a\ given\ time\ interval}{time\ interval}$$

The average speed is 48 feet per second: $\frac{144}{3} = 48$. *This is different than the average speed calculated in Example 1. In Example 1, the average speed over an interval of 3 seconds was 64 feet per second.*

4. Take a closer look at the data for the falling stone by answering the questions below.

   a. How many feet did the stone drop between 0 and 1 second?

   The stone dropped 16 feet between 0 and 1 second.

   b. How many feet did the stone drop between 1 and 2 seconds?

   The stone dropped 48 feet between 1 and 2 seconds.

   c. How many feet did the stone drop between 2 and 3 seconds?

   The stone dropped 80 feet between 2 and 3 seconds.

   d. How many feet did the stone drop between 3 and 4 seconds?

   The stone dropped 112 feet between 3 and 4 seconds.

   e. Compare the distances the stone dropped from one time interval to the next. What do you notice?

   Over each interval, the difference in the distance was 32 feet. For example, $16 + 32 = 48$, $48 + 32 = 80$, *and* $80 + 32 = 112$.

5. What is the average speed of the stone in each interval 0.5 seconds? For example, the average speed over the interval from 3.5 seconds to 4 seconds is

$$\frac{distance\ traveled\ over\ a\ given\ time\ interval}{time\ interval} = \frac{256 - 196}{4 - 3.5} = \frac{60}{0.5} = 120\ feet\ per\ second$$

Repeat this process for every half-second interval. Then answer the question that follows.

   a. Interval between 0 and 0.5 seconds:

   $$\frac{4}{0.5} = 8\ feet\ per\ second$$

   b. Interval between 0.5 and 1 seconds:

   $$\frac{12}{0.5} = 24\ feet\ per\ second$$

   c. Interval between 1 and 1.5 seconds:

   $$\frac{20}{0.5} = 40\ feet\ per\ second$$

   d. Interval between 1.5 and 2 seconds:

   $$\frac{28}{0.5} = 56\ feet\ per\ second$$

e.   Interval between 2 and 2.5 seconds:

$$\frac{36}{0.5} = 72 \text{ feet per second}$$

f.   Interval between 2.5 and 3 seconds:

$$\frac{44}{0.5} = 88 \text{ feet per second}$$

g.   Interval between 3 and 3.5 seconds:

$$\frac{52}{0.5} = 104 \text{ feet per second}$$

h.   Compare the average speed between each time interval. What do you notice?

Over each interval, there is an increase in the average speed of 16 feet per second. For example,

$8 + 16 = 24, \ 24 + 16 = 40, \ 40 + 16 = 56,$ *and so on.*

6.   Is there any pattern to the data of the falling stone? Record your thoughts below.

Time of Interval in seconds (t)	1	2	3	4
Distance Stone Fell in feet (y)	16	64	144	256

Accept any reasonable patterns that students notice as long as they can justify their claim. In the next lesson, students will learn that $y = 16t^2$.

Each distance has 16 as a factor. For example, $16 = 1(16), \ 64 = 4(16), \ 144 = 9(16),$ and $256 = 16(16).$

Closing (4 minutes)

Summarize, or ask students to summarize, the main points from the lesson:

- We know that we cannot always assume that a motion is a constant rate.
- We know that a function can be used to describe a motion over any time interval, even the very small time intervals, such as 1.00001.

Lesson Summary

Functions are used to make predictions about real life situations. For example, a function allows you to predict the distance an object has traveled for *any* given time interval.

Constant rate cannot always be assumed. If not stated clearly, you can look at various intervals and inspect the average speed. When the average speed is the same over all time intervals, then you have constant rate. When the average speed is different, you do not have a constant rate.

$$Average\ Speed = \frac{distance\ traveled\ over\ a\ given\ time\ interval}{time\ interval}$$

Exit Ticket (5 minutes)

Name _____   Date _____

Lesson 1: The Concept of a Function

Exit Ticket

1. A ball bounces across the schoolyard. It hits the ground at $(0,0)$ and bounces up and lands at $(1,0)$ and bounces again. The graph shows only one bounce.

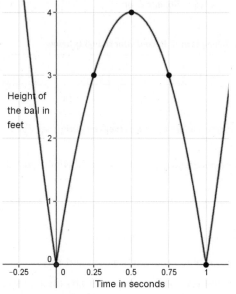

Height of the ball in feet

Time in seconds

a. Identify the height of the ball at the following values of t: 0, 0.25, 0.5, 0.75, 1.

b. What is the average speed of the ball over the first 0.25 seconds? What is the average speed of the ball over the next 0.25 seconds (from 0.25 to 0.5 seconds)?

c. Is the height of the ball changing at a constant rate?

Exit Ticket Sample Solutions

1. A ball is bouncing across the schoolyard. It hits the ground at $(0, 0)$ and bounces up and lands at $(1, 0)$ and bounces again. The graph shows only one bounce.

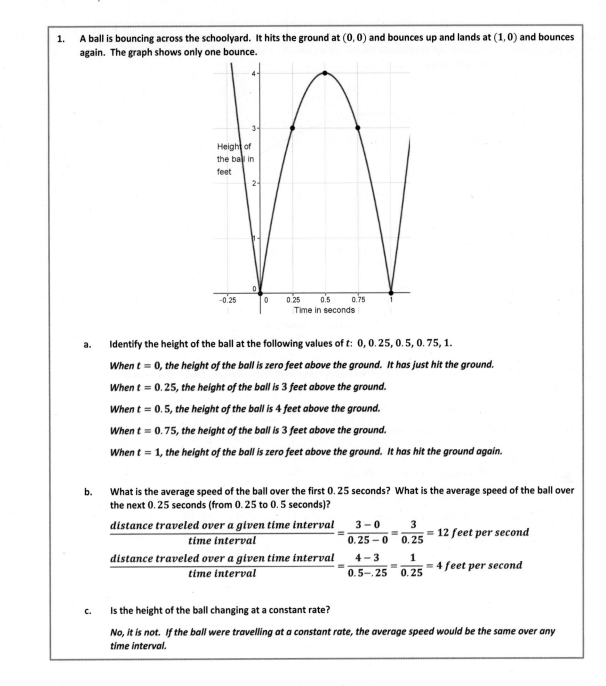

a. Identify the height of the ball at the following values of t: $0, 0.25, 0.5, 0.75, 1$.

When $t = 0$, the height of the ball is zero feet above the ground. It has just hit the ground.

When $t = 0.25$, the height of the ball is 3 feet above the ground.

When $t = 0.5$, the height of the ball is 4 feet above the ground.

When $t = 0.75$, the height of the ball is 3 feet above the ground.

When $t = 1$, the height of the ball is zero feet above the ground. It has hit the ground again.

b. What is the average speed of the ball over the first 0.25 seconds? What is the average speed of the ball over the next 0.25 seconds (from 0.25 to 0.5 seconds)?

$$\frac{distance\ traveled\ over\ a\ given\ time\ interval}{time\ interval} = \frac{3 - 0}{0.25 - 0} = \frac{3}{0.25} = 12\ feet\ per\ second$$

$$\frac{distance\ traveled\ over\ a\ given\ time\ interval}{time\ interval} = \frac{4 - 3}{0.5 - .25} = \frac{1}{0.25} = 4\ feet\ per\ second$$

c. Is the height of the ball changing at a constant rate?

No, it is not. If the ball were travelling at a constant rate, the average speed would be the same over any time interval.

Problem Set Sample Solutions

1. A ball is thrown across the field from point A to point B. It hits the ground at point B. The path of the ball is shown in the diagram below. The x-axis shows the distance the ball travels and the y-axis shows the height of the ball. Use the diagram to complete parts (a)-(g).

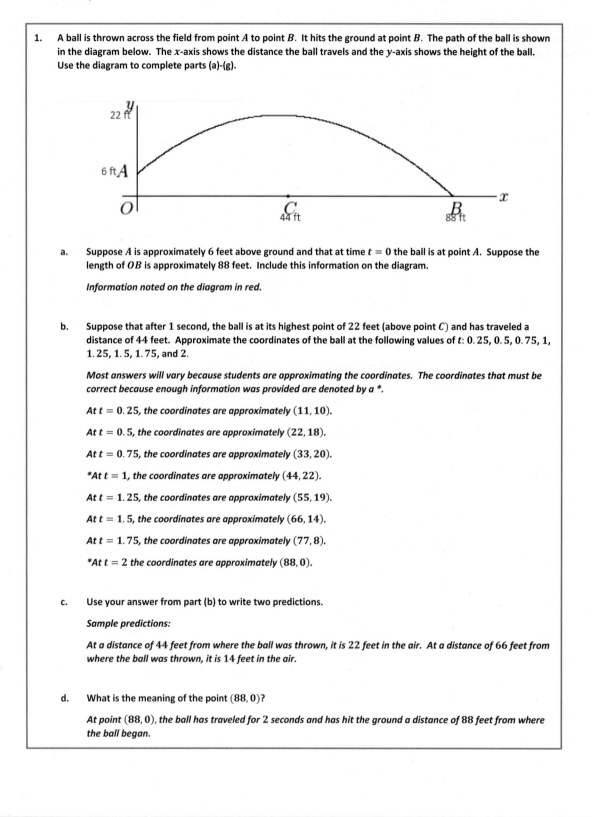

a. Suppose A is approximately 6 feet above ground and that at time $t = 0$ the ball is at point A. Suppose the length of OB is approximately 88 feet. Include this information on the diagram.

Information noted on the diagram in red.

b. Suppose that after 1 second, the ball is at its highest point of 22 feet (above point C) and has traveled a distance of 44 feet. Approximate the coordinates of the ball at the following values of t: $0.25, 0.5, 0.75, 1,$ $1.25, 1.5, 1.75,$ and 2.

Most answers will vary because students are approximating the coordinates. The coordinates that must be correct because enough information was provided are denoted by a *.

At $t = 0.25$, the coordinates are approximately $(11, 10)$.

At $t = 0.5$, the coordinates are approximately $(22, 18)$.

At $t = 0.75$, the coordinates are approximately $(33, 20)$.

*At $t = 1$, the coordinates are approximately $(44, 22)$.

At $t = 1.25$, the coordinates are approximately $(55, 19)$.

At $t = 1.5$, the coordinates are approximately $(66, 14)$.

At $t = 1.75$, the coordinates are approximately $(77, 8)$.

*At $t = 2$ the coordinates are approximately $(88, 0)$.

c. Use your answer from part (b) to write two predictions.

Sample predictions:

At a distance of 44 feet from where the ball was thrown, it is 22 feet in the air. At a distance of 66 feet from where the ball was thrown, it is 14 feet in the air.

d. What is the meaning of the point $(88, 0)$?

At point $(88, 0)$, the ball has traveled for 2 seconds and has hit the ground a distance of 88 feet from where the ball began.

e. Why do you think the ball is at point $(0, 6)$ when $t = 0$? In other words, why isn't the height of the ball zero?

The ball is thrown from point A to point B. The fact that the ball is at a height of 6 feet means that the person throwing it must have released the ball from a height of 6 feet.

f. Does the graph allow us to make predictions about the height of the ball at all points?

While we cannot predict exactly, the graph allows us to make approximate predictions of the height for any value of horizontal distance we choose.

2. In your own words, explain the purpose of a function and why it is needed.

A function allows us to make predictions about a motion without relying on the assumption of constant rate. It is needed because the entire story of the movement of an object cannot be told with just a few data points. There are an infinite number of points in time in which a distance can be recorded and a function allows us to calculate each one.

Lesson 1:   The Concept of a Function

Lesson 2: Formal Definition of a Function

Student Outcomes

- Students know that a function assigns to each input exactly one output.
- Students know that some functions can be expressed by a formula or rule, and when an input is used with the formula, the outcome is the output.

Lesson Notes

A function is defined as a rule (or formula) that assigns to each input exactly one output. Functions can be represented in a table, as a rule, as a formula or equation, as a graph, or as a verbal description. The word function will be used to describe a predictive relationship. That relationship is described with a rule or formula when possible. Students should also know that frequently the word function is used to mean the formula or equation representation, specifically.

This lesson continues the work of Example 2 from Lesson 1 leading to a formal definition of a function. Consider asking students to recap what they learned about functions from Lesson 1. The purpose would be to abstract the information in Example 2. Specifically, that in order to show all possible time intervals for the stone dropping we had to write the inequality for time t as $0 \le t \le 4$.

Classwork

Opening (3 minutes)

- Shown below are the table from Example 2 of the last lesson and another table of values. Make a conjecture about the differences between the two tables. What do you notice?

Number of seconds (x)	Distance traveled in feet (y)
0.5	4
1	16
1.5	36
2	64
2.5	100
3	144
3.5	196
4	256

Number of seconds (x)	Distance traveled in feet (y)
0.5	4
1	4
1	36
2	64
2.5	80
3	99
3	196
4	256

Allow students to share their conjectures about the differences between the two tables. Then proceed with the discussion that follows.

Discussion (8 minutes)

- Using the table on the left (above), predict the distance the stone traveled in 1 second?
  - *After 1 second the stone traveled 16 feet.*
- Using the table on the right (above), predict the distance the stone traveled in 1 second?
  - *After 1 second the stone traveled 4 or 36 feet.*
- Which of the two tables above allows us to make predictions with some accuracy? Explain.
  - *The table on the left seems like it would be more accurate. The table on the right gives two completely different distances for the stone after 1 second. We cannot make an accurate prediction because after 1 second the stone may either be 4 feet from where it started, or 36 feet.*
- The importance of a function is that we can immediately point to the position of the stone at exactly t seconds after the stone's release from a height of 256 feet. It is the ability to *assign*, or *associate*, the distance the stone has traveled to each t at time t from 256 feet that truly matters. For that reason, the table on the left describes a function, whereas the table on the right does not.
- Let's formalize this idea of *assignment* or *association* with a symbol, D, where "D" is used to suggest the distance of the fall. So, D assigns to each number t (where $0 \leq t \leq 4$) another number, which is the distance of the fall of the stone in t seconds. For example, we can rewrite the table from the last lesson as shown below:

Number of seconds (t)	Distance traveled in feet (y)
0.5	4
1	16
1.5	36
2	64
2.5	100
3	144
3.5	196
4	256

- We can also rewrite it as the following table which emphasizes the assignment the function makes to each input.

D assigns 4 to 0.5
D assigns 16 to 1
D assigns 36 to 1.5
D assigns 64 to 2
D assigns 100 to 2.5
D assigns 144 to 3
D assigns 196 to 3.5
D assigns 256 to 4

- Think of it as an *input-output machine*. That is, we put in a number (the input) that represents the time interval and out comes another number (the output) that tells us the distance that was traveled in feet during that particular interval.

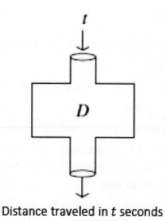

Distance traveled in t seconds

> Scaffolding:
>
> Highlighting the components of the words input and output and exploring how the words describe related concepts would be useful.

- With the example of the falling stone, what are we inputting?
  - *The input would be the time interval.*
- What is the output?
  - *The distance the stone traveled in the given time interval.*
- If we input 3 into the machine, what is the output?
  - *The output is 144.*
- If we input 1.5 into the machine, what is the output?
  - *The output is 36.*
- Of course with this particular machine we are limited to inputs in the range of 0 to 4 because we are inputting the time it took for the stone to fall, i.e., time t where $0 \le t \le 4$.

  The function D can be expressed by a formula in the sense that the number assigned to each t can be calculated with a mathematical expression, which is a property that is generally not shared by other functions. Thanks to Newtonian physics (Isaac Newton, think apple falling on your head from a tree), for a distance traveled in feet for a time interval of t seconds, the function can be expressed as the following:

$$\text{distance for time interval } t = 16t^2$$

- From your work in the last lesson, recall that you recognized 16 as a factor for each of the distances in the table below.

Time of Interval in seconds (t)	1	2	3	4
Distance Stone Fell in feet (y)	16	64	144	256

- Functions can be represented in a variety of ways. At this point we have seen the function that describes the distance traveled by the stone pictorially (from Lesson 1, Example 2), as a table of values, and as a rule. We could also provide a verbal description of the movement of the stone.

Lesson 2:   Formal Definition of a Function

Exercise 1 (5 minutes)

Have students verify that the function we are using to represent this situation is accurate by completing Exercise 1. To expedite the verification, consider allowing the use of calculators.

Exercise 1

1. Let y be the distance traveled in time t. Use the function $y = 16t^2$ to calculate the distance the stone dropped for the given time t.

Time of Interval in seconds (t)	0.5	1	1.5	2	2.5	3	3.5	4
Distance Stone Fell in feet (y)	4	16	36	64	100	144	196	256

  a. Are the distances you calculated equal to the table from Lesson 1?

    Yes.

  b. Does the function $y = 16t^2$ accurately represent the distance the stone fell after a given time t? In other words, does the function assign to t the correct distance? Explain.

    Yes, the function accurately represents the distance the stone fell after the given time interval. Each computation using the function resulted in the correct distance. Therefore, the function assigns to t the correct distance.

Discussion (10 minutes)

- Being able to write a formula for the function has fantastic implications—it is predictive. That is, we can predict in advance what will happen each time a stone is released from a height of 256 feet. The function makes it possible for us to know exactly how many feet the stone will fall for a time t as long as we select a t so that $0 \leq t \leq 4$.

- As stated before, not every function can be expressed as a formula. Imagine being able to write a formula that would allow you to predict the correct answers on a multiple choice test!

- Now that we have a little more background on functions, we can define them formally. A **function** is a rule (formula) that assigns to each input exactly one output.

- Let's examine that definition more closely. A function is a rule that assigns to each input *exactly one output.* Can you think of why the phrase "exactly one output" must be in the definition?

Provide time for students to consider the phrase. Allow them to talk in pairs or small groups then share their thoughts with the class. Use the question below, if necessary. Then resume the discussion.

- Using our stone dropping example, if D assigns 64 to 2, that is, the function assigns 64 feet to the time interval 2, would it be possible for D to assign 65 to 2 as well? Explain.

  □ *It would not be possible for D to assign 64 and 65 to 2. The reason is that we are talking about a stone dropping. How could the stone drop 64 feet in two seconds and 65 feet in 2 seconds? The stone cannot be in two places at once.*

- In order for functions to be useful, the information we get from a function must be useful. That is why a function assigns to each input exactly one output. We also need to consider the situation when using a function. For example, if we use the function, distance for time interval $t = 16t^2$, for $t = -2$, we may be able to explain that -2 would represent 2 seconds before the stone was dropped.

MP.6

Yet, in the function

$$\text{distance for time interval } t = 16t^2 \quad \text{for } t = -2$$
$$= 16(-2)^2$$
$$= 16(4)$$
$$= 64$$

we could conclude that the stone dropped a distance of 64 feet two seconds before the stone was dropped! Or consider the situation when $t = 5$:

$$\text{distance for time interval } t = 16t^2 \quad \text{for } t = 5$$
$$= 16(5)^2$$
$$= 16(25)$$
$$= 400$$

- What is wrong with this statement?
  - *It would mean that the stone dropped 400 feet in 5 seconds, but the stone was dropped from a height of 256 feet.*

- To summarize, a function is a rule that assigns to each input exactly one output. Additionally, we should always consider the context, if provided, when working with a function to make sure our answer makes sense. In many cases, functions are described by a formula. However, we will soon learn that the assignment of some functions cannot be described by a mathematical rule.

Exercises 2–5 (10 minutes)

Students work independently to complete Exercises 2–5.

Exercises 2–5

2. Can the table shown below represent a function? Explain.

Input (x)	1	3	5	5	9
Output (y)	7	16	19	20	28

No, the table cannot represent a function because the input of 5 has two different outputs. Functions assign only one output to each input.

3. Can the table shown below represent a function? Explain.

Input (x)	0.5	7	7	12	15
Output (y)	1	15	10	23	30

No, the table cannot represent a function because the input of 7 has two different outputs. Functions assign only one output to each input.

---

4. Can the table shown below represent a function? Explain.

Input (x)	10	20	50	75	90
Output (y)	32	32	156	240	288

Yes, the table can represent a function. Even though there are two outputs that are the same, each input has only one output.

5. It takes Josephine 34 minutes to complete her homework assignment of 10 problems. If we assume that she works at a constant rate, we can describe the situation using a function.

a. Predict how many problems Josephine can complete in 25 minutes.

Answers will vary.

b. Write the two-variable linear equation that represents Josephine's constant rate of work.

Let y be the number of problems she can complete in x minutes.

$$\frac{10}{34} = \frac{y}{x}$$

$$y = \frac{10}{34}x$$

$$y = \frac{5}{17}x$$

c. Use the equation you wrote in part (b) as the formula for the function to complete the table below. Round your answers to the hundredths place.

Time taken to complete problems (x)	5	10	15	20	25
Number of problems completed (y)	1.47	2.94	4.41	5.88	7.35

After 5 minutes, Josephine was able to complete 1.47 problems, which means that she was able to complete 1 problem, then get about halfway through the next problem.

d. Compare your prediction from part (a) to the number you found in the table above.

Answers will vary.

e. Use the formula from part (b) to compute the number of problems completed when $x = -7$. Does your answer make sense? Explain.

$$y = \frac{5}{17}(-7)$$

$$= -2.06$$

No, the answer does not make sense in terms of the situation. The answer means that Josephine can complete -2.06 problems in -7 minutes. This obviously does not make sense.

f. For this problem we assumed that Josephine worked at a constant rate. Do you think that is a reasonable assumption for this situation? Explain.

It does not seem reasonable to assume constant rate for this situation. Just because Josephine was able to complete 10 problems in 34 minutes does not necessarily mean she spent the exact same amount of time on each problem. For example, it may have taken her 20 minutes to do one problem and then 14 minutes total to finish the remaining 9 problems.

Closing (4 minutes)

Summarize, or ask students to summarize, the main points from the lesson:

- We know that a function is a rule or formula that assigns to each input exactly one output.
- We know that not every function can be expressed by a mathematical rule or formula. The rule or formula can be a description of the assignment.
- We know that functions have limitations with respect to the situation they describe. For example, we cannot determine the distance a stone drops in -2 seconds.

Lesson Summary

A <u>function</u> is a rule that assigns to each input <u>*exactly one output.*</u> The phrase "exactly one output" must be part of the definition so that the function can serve its purpose of being predictive.

Functions are sometimes described as an *input-output machine*. For example, given a function D, the input is time t and the output is the distance traveled in t seconds.

t

D

Distance traveled in t seconds

Exit Ticket (5 minutes)

Lesson 2:   Formal Definition of a Function

Name _____   Date _____

Lesson 2: Formal Definition of a Function

Exit Ticket

1. Can the table shown below represent a function? Explain.

Input (x)	10	20	30	40	50
Output (y)	32	64	96	64	32

2. Kelly can tune up four cars in three hours. If we assume he works at a constant rate, we can describe the situation using a function.

    a. Write the rule that describes the function that represents Kelly's constant rate of work.

    b. Use the function you wrote in part (a) as the formula for the function to complete the table below. Round your answers to the hundredths place.

Time it takes to tune up cars (x)	2	3	4	6	7
Number of cars tuned up (y)					

    c. Kelly works 8 hours per day. How many cars will he finish tuning up at the end of a shift?

    d. For this problem we assumed that Kelly worked at a constant rate. Do you think that is a reasonable assumption for this situation? Explain.

Exit Ticket Sample Solutions

1. Can the table shown below represent a function? Explain.

Input (x)	10	20	30	40	50
Output (y)	32	64	96	64	32

Yes, the table can represent a function. Each input has exactly one output.

2. Kelly can tune up four cars in three hours. If we assume he works at a constant rate, we can describe the situation using a function.

    a. Write the function that represents Kelly's constant rate of work.

    Let y represent the number of cars Kelly can tune up in x hours, then

$$\frac{y}{x} = \frac{4}{3}$$
$$y = \frac{4}{3}x$$

    b. Use the function you wrote in part (a) as the formula for the function to complete the table below. Round your answers to the hundredths place.

Time it takes to tune up cars (x)	2	3	4	6	7
Number of cars tuned up (y)	2.67	4	5.33	8	9.33

    c. Kelly works 8 hours per day. How many cars will he finish tuning up at the end of a shift?

    Using the function, Kelly will tune up 10.67 cars at the end of his shift. That means he will finish tuning up 10 cars and begin tuning up the 11th car.

    d. For this problem we assumed that Kelly worked at a constant rate. Do you think that is a reasonable assumption for this situation? Explain.

    No, it does not seem reasonable to assume a constant rate for this situation. Just because Kelly tuned up 4 cars in 3 hours does not mean he spent the exact same amount of time on each car. One car could have taken 1 hour, while the other three could have taken 2 hours total.

Problem Set Sample Solutions

1. The table below represents the number of minutes Francisco spends at the gym each day for a week. Does the data shown below represent a function? Explain.

Day (x)	1	2	3	4	5	6	7
Time in minutes (y)	35	45	30	45	35	0	0

Yes, the table can represent a function because each input has a unique output. For example, on day 1, Francisco was at the gym for 35 minutes.

2. Can the table shown below represent a function? Explain.

Input (x)	9	8	7	8	9
Output (y)	11	15	19	24	28

No, the table cannot represent a function because the input of 9 has two different outputs and so does the input of 8. Functions assign only one output to each input.

3. Olivia examined the table of values shown below and stated that a possible rule to describe this function could be $y = -2x + 9$. Is she correct? Explain.

Input (x)	−4	0	4	8	12	16	20	24
Output (y)	17	9	1	−7	−15	−23	−31	−39

Yes, Olivia is correct. When the rule is used with each input, the value of the output is exactly what is shown in the table. Therefore, the rule for this function must be $y = -2x + 9$.

4. Peter said that the set of data in part (a) describes a function, but the set of data in part (b) does not. Do you agree? Explain why or why not.

a.

Input (x)	1	2	3	4	5	6	7	8
Output (y)	8	10	32	6	10	27	156	4

b.

Input (x)	−6	−15	−9	−3	−2	−3	8	9
Output (y)	0	−6	8	14	1	2	11	41

Peter is correct. The table in part (a) fits the definition of a function. That is, there is exactly one output for each input. The table in part (b) cannot be a function. The input −3 has two outputs, 14 and 2. This contradicts the definition of a function; therefore, it is not a function.

5. A function can be described by the rule $y = x^2 + 4$. Determine the corresponding output for each given input.

Input (x)	−3	−2	−1	0	1	2	3	4
Output (y)	13	8	5	4	5	8	13	20

6. Examine the data in the table below. The inputs and outputs represent a situation where constant rate can be assumed. Determine the rule that describes the function.

Input (x)	−1	0	1	2	3	4	5	6
Output (y)	3	8	13	18	23	28	33	38

The rule that describes this function is $y = 5x + 8$.

Lesson 2:   Formal Definition of a Function

7. Examine the data in the table below. The inputs represent the number of bags of candy purchased, and the outputs represent the cost. Determine the cost of one bag of candy, assuming the price per bag is the same no matter how much candy is purchased. Then, complete the table.

Bags of Candy (x)	1	2	3	4	5	6	7	8
Cost (y)	$1.25	$2.50	$3.75	$5	$6.25	$7.50	$8.75	$10

a. Write the rule that describes the function.

$y = 1.25x$

b. Can you determine the value of the output for an input of $x = -4$? If so, what is it?

When $x = -4$, the output is -5.

c. Does an input of -4 make sense in this situation? Explain.

No, an input of -4 does not make sense for the situation. It would mean -4 bags of candy. You cannot purchase -4 bags of candy.

8. A local grocery store sells 2 pounds of bananas for $1. Can this situation be represented by a function? Explain.

Yes, this situation can be represented by a function if the cost of 2 pounds of banana is $1. That is, at all times the cost of 2 pounds will be one dollar, not any more or any less. The function assigns the cost of $1 to 2 pounds of bananas.

9. Write a brief explanation to a classmate who was absent today about why the table in part (a) is a function and the table in part (b) is not.

a.

Input (x)	-1	-2	-3	-4	4	3	2	1
Output (y)	81	100	320	400	400	320	100	81

b.

Input (x)	1	6	-9	-2	1	-10	8	14
Output (y)	2	6	-47	-8	19	-2	15	31

The table in part (a) is a function because each input has exactly one output. This is different from the information in the table in part (b). Notice that the input of 1 has been assigned two different values. The input of 1 is assigned 2 and 19. Because the input of 1 has more than one output, this table cannot represent a function.

EUREKA MATH

Lesson 2:   Formal Definition of a Function

Lesson 3: Linear Functions and Proportionality

Student Outcomes

- Students relate constant speed and proportional relationships to linear functions using information from a table.
- Students know that distance traveled is a function of the time spent traveling and that the total cost of an item is a function of how many items are purchased.

Classwork

Example 1 (7 minutes)

Example 1

In the last lesson we looked at several tables of values that represented the inputs and outputs of functions. For example:

Bags of Candy (x)	1	2	3	4	5	6	7	8
Cost (y)	$1.25	$2.50	$3.75	$5	$6.25	$7.50	$8.75	$10

- What do you think a *linear* function is?
  - *A linear function is likely a function with a linear relationship. Specifically, the rate of change is constant and the graph is a line.*
- In the last lesson, we looked at several tables of values that represented the inputs and outputs of functions. For example:

Bags of Candy (x)	1	2	3	4	5	6	7	8
Cost (y)	$1.25	$2.50	$3.75	$5	$6.25	$7.50	$8.75	$10

- Do you think this is a *linear* function? Justify your answer.
  - *Yes, this is a linear function because there is a constant rate of change, as shown below:*

$$\frac{\$10}{8\ bags\ of\ candy} = \$1.25\ per\ each\ bag\ of\ candy$$

$$\frac{\$5}{4\ bags\ of\ candy} = \$1.25\ per\ each\ bag\ of\ candy$$

$$\frac{\$2.50}{2\ bags\ of\ candy} = \$1.25\ per\ each\ bag\ of\ candy$$

Scaffolding:

In addition to explanations about functions, it may be useful for students to have a series of structured experiences with real-world objects and data to reinforce their understanding of a function. An example is experimenting with different numbers of "batches" of a given recipe; students can observe the effect of the number of batches on quantities of various ingredients.

□ *The total cost is increasing at a rate of* $1.25 *with each bag of candy. Further proof comes from the graph of the data shown below.*

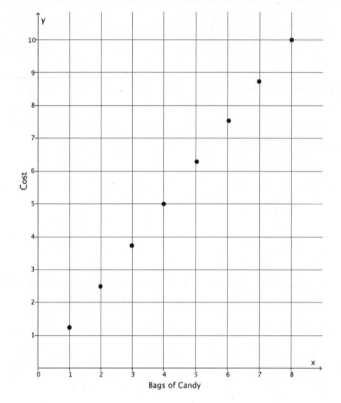

- A linear function is a function with a rule so that the output is equal to m multiplied by the input plus b, where m and b are fixed constants. If y is the output and x is the input, then a linear function is represented by the rule $y = mx + b$. That is, when the rule that describes the function is in the form of $y = mx + b$, then the function is a linear function. Notice that this is not any different from a linear equation in two variables. What rule or equation describes this function?

    □ *The rule that represents the function is then* $y = 1.25x$.

- Notice that the constant m is 1.25, which is the cost of one bag of candy, and the constant b is zero. Also notice that the constant m was found by calculating the unit rate for a bag of candy. What we know of linear functions so far is no different than what we learned about linear equations—the unit rate of a proportional relationship is the rate of change.

- No matter what value of x is chosen, as long as x is a non-negative integer, the rule $y = 1.25x$ represents the cost function of a bag of candy. Moreover, *the total cost of candy is a function of the number of bags purchased.*

- Why do we have to note that x is a non-negative integer for this function?

    □ *Since x represents the number of bags of candy, it does not make sense that there would be a negative number of bags. For that reason, x as a positive integer means the function allows us to find the cost of zero or more bags of candy.*

- Would you say that the table represents all possible inputs and outputs? Explain.

    □ *No, it does not represent all possible inputs and outputs. I'm sure someone can purchase more than* 8 *bags of candy, and inputs greater than* 8 *are not represented by this table.*

Lesson 3:   Linear Functions and Proportionality

- As a matter of precision, we say that "this function has the above table of values" instead of "the table above represents a function" because not all values of the function can be represented by the table. The rule, or formula, that describes the function can represent all of the possible values of a function. For example, using the rule we could determine the cost for 9 bags of candy. However, this statement should not lead you to believe that a table cannot entirely represent a function. In this context, if there were a limit on the number of bags that could be purchased, i.e., 8 bags, then the table above would represent the function completely.

Example 2 (4 minutes)

> **Example 2**
>
> Walter walks 8 miles in two hours. What is his average speed?

- Consider the following rate problem: Walter walks 8 miles in two hours. What is his average speed?

  □ *Walter's average speed of walking 8 miles is $\frac{8}{2} = 4$, or 4 miles per hour.*

> *Scaffolding:*
>
> As the language becomes more abstract, it can be useful to use visuals and even pantomime situations related to speed, rate, etc.

- If we assume constant speed, then we can determine the distance Walter walks over any time period using the equation $y = 4x$, where y is the distance walked in x hours. Walter's rate of walking is constant; therefore, no matter what x is, we can say that the distance Walter walks is a linear function given by the equation $y = 4x$. Again, notice that the constant m of $y = mx + b$ is 4, which represents the unit rate of walking for Walter.

- In the last example, the total cost of candy was a function of the number of bags purchased. Describe the function in this example.

  □ *The distance that Walter travels is a function of the number of hours he spends walking.*

- What limitations do we need to put on x?

  □ *The limitation that we should put on x is that $x \geq 0$. Since x represents the time Walter walks, then it makes sense that he would walk for a positive amount of time or no time at all.*

- Since x is positive, then we know that the distance y will also be positive.

Example 3 (4 minutes)

> **Example 3**
>
> Veronica runs at a constant speed. The distance she runs is a function of the time she spends running. The function has the table of values shown below.
>
> | Time in Minutes (x) | 8 | 16 | 24 | 32 |
> |---|---|---|---|---|
> | Distance Ran in Miles (y) | 1 | 2 | 3 | 4 |

- Veronica runs at a constant speed. The distance she runs is a function of the time she spends running. The function has the table of values shown below.

Time in Minutes (x)	8	16	24	32
Distance Ran in Miles (y)	1	2	3	4

- Since Veronica runs at a constant speed, we know that her average speed over any time interval will be the same. Therefore, Veronica's distance function is a linear function. Write the equation that describes her distance function.

    ▫ *The function that represents Veronica's distance is described by the equation $y = \frac{1}{8}x$, where y is the distance in miles Veronica runs in x minutes and $x, y \geq 0$.*

- Describe the function in terms of distance and time.

    ▫ *The distance that Veronica runs is a function of the number of minutes she spends running.*

Example 4 (5 minutes)

Example 4

Water flows from a faucet at a constant rate. That is, the volume of water that flows out of the faucet is the same over any given time interval. If 7 gallons of water flow from the faucet every 2 minutes, determine the rule that describes the volume function of the faucet.

The rate of water flow is $\frac{7}{2}$, 3.5 gallons per minute. Then the rule that describes the volume function of the faucet is $y = 3.5x$, where y is the volume of water that flows from the faucet and x is the number of minutes the faucet is on.

- Assume that the faucet is filling a bathtub that can hold 50 gallons of water. How long will it take the faucet to fill the tub?

    ▫ *Since we want the total volume to be 50 gallons, then*

    $$50 = 3.5x$$

    $$\frac{50}{3.5} = x$$

    $$14.2857\ldots = x$$

    $$14 \approx x$$

    It will take about 14 minutes to fill a tub that has a volume of 50 gallons.

Now assume that you are filling the same tub, a tub with a volume of 50 gallons, with the same faucet, a faucet where the rate of water flow is 3.5 gallons per minute. This time, however, the tub already has 8 gallons in it. Will it still take 14 minutes to fill the tub? Explain.

No, it will take less time because there is already some water in the tub.

- How can we reflect the water that is already in the tub with our volume of water flow as a function of time for the faucet?
  - *If y is the volume of water that flows from the faucet and x is the number of minutes the faucet is on, then $y = 3.5x + 8$.*
- How long will it take the faucet to fill the tub if the tub already has 8 gallons in it?
  - *Since we still want the total volume of the tub to be 50 gallons, then*

$$50 = 3.5x + 8$$
$$42 = 3.5x$$
$$12 = x$$

  It will take 12 minutes for the faucet to fill a 50 gallon tub when 8 gallons are already in it.
- Generate a table of values for this function:

Time in Minutes (x)	0	3	6	9	12
Total Volume in Tub in Gallons (y)	8	18.5	29	39.5	50

Example 5 (7 minutes)

Example 5

Water flows from a faucet at a constant rate. Assume that 6 gallons of water are already in a tub by the time we notice the faucet is on. This information is recorded as 0 minutes and 6 gallons of water in the table below. The other values show how many gallons of water are in the tub at the given number of minutes.

Time in Minutes (x)	0	3	5	9
Total Volume in Tub in Gallons (y)	6	9.6	12	16.8

- After 3 minutes pass, there are 9.6 gallons in the tub. How much water flowed from the faucet in those 3 minutes? Explain.
  - *Since there were already 6 gallons in the tub, after 3 minutes an additional 3.6 gallons filled the tub.*
- Use this information to determine the rate of water flow.
  - *In 3 minutes, 3.6 gallons were added to the tub, then $\frac{3.6}{3} = 1.2$, and the faucet fills the tub at a rate of 1.2 gallons per minute.*
- Verify that the rate of water flow is correct using the other values in the table.
  - *Sample student work:*
    $5(1.2) = 6$ and since 6 gallons were already in the tub, the total volume in the tub is 12 gallons.
    $9(1.2) = 10.8$ and since 6 gallons were already in the tub, the total volume in the tub is 16.8 gallons.
- Write the volume of water flow as a function of time that represents the rate of water flow from the faucet.
  - *The volume function that represents the rate of water flow from the faucet is $y = 1.2x$, where y is the volume of water that flows from the faucet and x is the number of minutes the faucet is on.*

- Write the rule or equation that describes the volume of water flow as a function of time for filling the tub, including the 6 gallons that are already in the tub to begin with.
    - *Since the tub already has 6 gallons it in, then the rule is $y = 1.2x + 6$.*
- How many minutes was the faucet on before we noticed it? Explain.
    - *Since 6 gallons were in the tub by the time we noticed the faucet was on, we need to determine how many minutes it takes for 6 gallons to flow from the faucet:*

$$6 = 1.2x$$
$$5 = x$$

The faucet was on for 5 minutes before we noticed it.

Exercises 1–3 (10 minutes)

Students complete Exercises 1–3 independently or in pairs.

Exercises 1–3

1. A linear function has the table of values below. The information in the table shows the function of time in minutes with respect to mowing an area of lawn in square feet.

Number of Minutes (x)	5	20	30	50
Area Mowed in Square Feet (y)	36	144	216	360

a. Explain why this is a linear function.

   Sample responses:

   Linear functions have a constant rate of change. When we compare the rates at each interval of time, they will be equal to the same constant.

   When the data is graphed on the coordinate plane, it appears to make a line.

b. Describe the function in terms of area mowed and time.

   The total area mowed is a function of the number of minutes spent mowing.

c. What is the rate of mowing a lawn in 5 minutes?

$$\frac{36}{5} = 7.2$$

   The rate is 7.2 square feet per minute.

d. What is the rate of mowing a lawn in 20 minutes?

$$\frac{144}{20} = 7.2$$

   The rate is 7.2 square feet per minute.

---

e. What is the rate for mowing a lawn in 30 minutes?

$$\frac{216}{30} = 7.2$$

The rate is 7.2 square feet per minute.

f. What is the rate for mowing a lawn in in 50 minutes?

$$\frac{360}{50} = 7.2$$

The rate is 7.2 square feet per minute.

g. Write the rule that represents the linear function that describes the area in square feet mowed, y, in x minutes.

$$y = 7.2x$$

h. Describe the limitations of x and y.

Both x and y must be positive numbers. The symbol x represents time spent mowing, which means it should be positive. Similarly, y represents the area mowed, which should also be positive.

i. What number does the function assign to 24? That is, what area of lawn can be mowed in 24 minutes?

$$y = 7.2(24)$$
$$y = 172.8$$

In 24 minutes, an area of 172.8 square feet can be mowed.

j. How many minutes would it take to mow an area of 400 square feet?

$$400 = 7.2x$$
$$\frac{400}{7.2} = x$$
$$55.555\ldots = x$$
$$56 \approx x$$

It would take about 56 minutes to mow an area of 400 square feet.

2. A linear function has the table of values below. The information in the table shows the volume of water that flows from a hose in gallons as a function of time in minutes.

Time in Minutes (x)	10	25	50	70
Total Volume of Water in Gallons (y)	44	110	220	308

a. Describe the function in terms of volume and time.

The total volume of water that flows from a hose is a function of the number of minutes the hose is left on.

b. Write the rule that represents the linear function that describes the volume of water in gallons, y, in x minutes.

$$y = \frac{44}{10}x$$
$$y = 4.4x$$

c. What number does the function assign to 250? That is, how many gallons of water flow from the hose in 250 minutes?

$$y = 4.4(250)$$
$$y = 1,100$$

In 250 minutes, 1,100 gallons of water flow from the hose.

d. The average pool has about 17,300 gallons of water. The pool has already been filled $\frac{1}{4}$ of its volume. Write the rule that describes the volume of water flow as a function of time for filling the pool using the hose, including the number of gallons that are already in the pool.

$$\frac{1}{4}(17,300) = 4,325$$
$$y = 4.4x + 4,325$$

e. Approximately how much time, in hours, will it take to finish filling the pool?

$$17,300 = 4.4x + 4,325$$
$$12,975 = 4.4x$$
$$\frac{12,975}{4.4} = x$$
$$2,948.8636\ldots = x$$
$$2,949 \approx x$$

$$\frac{2,949}{60} = 49.15$$

It will take about 49 hours to fill the pool with the hose.

3. Recall that a linear function can be described by a rule in the form of $y = mx + b$, where m and b are constants. A particular linear function has the table of values below.

Input (x)	0	4	10	11	15	20	23
Output (y)	4	24	54	59	79	104	119

a. What is the equation that describes the function?

$$y = 5x + 4$$

b. Complete the table using the rule.

Closing (4 minutes)

Summarize, or ask students to summarize, the main points from the lesson:

- We know that a linear function can be described by a rule in the form of $y = mx + b$, where m and b are constants.
- We know that constant rates and proportional relationships can be described by a linear function.
- We know that the distance traveled is a function of the time spent traveling, that the volume of water flow from a faucet is a function of the time the faucet is on, etc.

Lesson Summary

Functions can be described by a rule in the form of $y = mx + b$, where m and b are constants.

Constant rates and proportional relationships can be described by a function, specifically a linear function where the rule is a linear equation.

Functions are described in terms of their inputs and outputs. For example, if the inputs are related to time and the output are distances traveled at given time intervals then we say that the distance traveled is a function of the time spent traveling.

Exit Ticket (4 minutes)

Lesson 3:   Linear Functions and Proportionality

Name _____   Date _____

Lesson 3: Linear Functions and Proportionality

1. A linear function has the table of values below. The information in the tables shows the number of pages a student can read in a certain book as a function of time in minutes. Assume a constant rate.

Time in Minutes (x)	2	6	11	20
Total Number of Pages Read in a Certain Book (y)	7	21	38.5	70

a. Write the rule or equation that represents the linear function that describes the total number of pages read, y, in x minutes.

b. How many pages can be read in 45 minutes?

c. This certain book has 396 pages. The student has already read $\frac{3}{8}$ of the pages. Write the equation that describes the number of pages read as a function of time for reading this book, including the number pages that have already been read.

d. Approximately how much time, in minutes, will it take to finish reading the book?

Exit Ticket Sample Solutions

1. A linear function has the table of values below. The information in the tables shows the number of pages a student can read in a certain book as a function of time in minutes. Assume a constant rate.

Time in Minutes (x)	2	6	11	20
Total Number of Pages Read in a Certain Book (y)	7	21	38.5	70

a. Write the rule or equation that represents the linear function that describes the total number of pages read, y, in x minutes.

$$y = \frac{7}{2}x$$
$$y = 3.5x$$

b. How many pages can be read in 45 minutes?

$$y = 3.5(45)$$
$$y = 157.5$$

In 45 minutes, the student can read 157.5 pages.

c. This certain book has 396 pages. The student has already read $\frac{3}{8}$ of the pages. Write the equation that describes the number of pages read as a function of time for reading this book, including the number pages that have already been read.

$$\frac{3}{8}(396) = 148.5$$
$$y = 3.5x + 148.5$$

d. Approximately how much time, in minutes, will it take to finish reading the book?

$$398 = 3.5x + 148.5$$
$$249.5 = 3.5x$$
$$\frac{249.5}{3.5} = x$$
$$71.285714\ldots = x$$
$$71 \approx x$$

It will take about 71 minutes to finish reading the book.

Problem Set Sample Solutions

1. A food bank distributes cans of vegetables every Saturday. They keep track of the cans in the following manner in the table. A linear function can be used to represent the data. The information in the table shows the function of time in weeks to the number of cans of vegetables distributed by the food bank.

Number of Weeks (x)	1	12	20	45
Number of Cans of Vegetables Distributed (y)	180	2,160	3,600	8,100

a. Describe the function in terms of cans distributed and time.

   The total number of cans handed out is a function of the number of weeks that pass.

b. Write the equation or rule that represents the linear function that describes the number of cans handed out, y, in x weeks.

$$y = \frac{180}{1}x$$
$$y = 180x$$

c. Assume that the food bank wants to distribute $20,000$ cans of vegetables. How long will it take them to meet that goal?

$$20,000 = 180x$$
$$\frac{20,000}{180} = x$$
$$111.1111\ldots = x$$
$$111 \approx x$$

   It will take about 111 weeks to distribute 20,000 cans of vegetables or about 2 years.

d. Assume that the food bank has already handed out $35,000$ cans of vegetables and continues to hand out cans at the same rate each week. Write a linear function that accounts for the number of cans already handed out.

$$y = 180x + 35,000$$

e. Using your function in part (c), determine how long in years it will take the food bank to hand out $80,000$ cans of vegetables.

$$80,000 = 180x + 35,000$$
$$45,000 = 180x$$
$$\frac{45,000}{180} = x$$
$$250 = x$$
$$\frac{250}{52} = number\ of\ years$$
$$4.8076\ldots = number\ of\ years$$
$$4.8 \approx number\ of\ years$$

   It will take about 4.8 years to distribute 80,000 cans of vegetables.

2. A linear function has the table of values below. The information in the table shows the function of time in hours to the distance an airplane travels in miles. Assume constant speed.

Number of Hour Traveled (x)	2.5	4	4.2
Distance in Miles (y)	1,062.5	1700	1,785

a. Describe the function in terms of distance and time.

The total distance traveled is a function of the number of hours spent flying.

b. Write the rule that represents the linear function that describes the distance traveled in miles, y, in x hours.

$$y = \frac{1,062.5}{2.5}x$$
$$y = 425x$$

c. Assume that the airplane is making a trip from New York to Los Angeles which is approximately $2,475$ miles. How long will it take the airplane to get to Los Angeles?

$$2,475 = 425x$$
$$\frac{2,475}{425} = x$$
$$5.82352\ldots = x$$
$$5.8 \approx x$$

It will take about 5.8 hours for the airplane to fly $2,475$ miles.

d. The airplane flies for 8 hours. How many miles will it be able to travel in that time interval?

$$y = 425(8)$$
$$y = 3,400$$

The airplane would travel $3,400$ miles in 8 hours.

3. A linear function has the table of values below. The information in the table shows the function of time in hours to the distance a car travels in miles.

Number of Hours Traveled (x)	3.5	3.75	4	4.25
Distance in Miles (y)	203	217.5	232	246.5

a. Describe the function in terms of area distance and time.

The total distance traveled is a function of the number of hours spent traveling.

b. Write the rule that represents the linear function that describes the distance traveled in miles, y, in x hours.

$$y = \frac{203}{3.5}x$$
$$y = 58x$$

c. Assume that the person driving the car is going on a road trip that is 500 miles from their starting point. How long will it take them to get to their destination?

$$500 = 58x$$
$$\frac{500}{58} = x$$
$$8.6206\ldots = x$$
$$8.6 \approx x$$

It will take about 8.6 hours to travel 500 miles.

d. Assume that a second car is going on the road trip from the same starting point and traveling at the same rate. However, this car has already driven 210 miles. Write the rule that represents the linear function that accounts for the miles already driven by this car.

$$y = 58x + 210$$

e. How long will it take the second car to drive the remainder of the trip?

$$500 = 58x + 210$$
$$290 = 58x$$
$$\frac{290}{58} = x$$
$$5 = x$$

It will take 5 hours to drive the remaining 290 miles of the road trip.

4. A particular linear function has the table of values below.

Input (x)	2	3	8	11	15	20	23
Output (y)	7	10	25	34	46	61	70

a. What is the equation that describes the function?

$$y = 3x + 1$$

b. Complete the table using the rule.

5. A particular linear function has the table of values below.

Input (x)	0	5	8	13	15	18	21
Output (y)	6	11	14	19	21	24	27

a. What is the rule that describes the function?

$$y = x + 6$$

b. Complete the table using the rule.

Lesson 4: More Examples of Functions

Student Outcomes

- Students examine and recognize real-world functions, such as the cost of a book, as discrete rates.
- Students examine and recognize real-world functions, such as the temperature of a pot of cooling soup, as continuous rates.

Classwork

Discussion (5 minutes)

- In the last couple of lessons we looked at several linear functions and the numbers that are assigned by the function in the form of a table.

Table A:

Bags of Candy (x)	1	2	3	4	5	6	7	8
Cost (y)	$1.25	$2.50	$3.75	$5	$6.25	$7.50	$8.75	$10

Table B:

Number of Seconds (x)	0.5	1	1.5	2	2.5	3	3.5	4
Distance Traveled in Feet (y)	4	16	36	64	100	144	196	256

In Table A, the context was purchasing bags of candy. In Table B, it was the distance traveled by a moving object. Examine the tables. What are the differences between these two situations?

Provide time for students to discuss the differences between the two tables and share their thoughts with the class. Then continue with the discussion below.

- For the function in Table A, we said that the rule that described the function was $y = 1.25x$, where $x \geq 0$.
- Why did we restrict x to numbers equal to or greater than zero?
  - *We restricted x to numbers equal to or greater than zero because you cannot purchase -1 bags of candy, for example.*
- If we assume that only a whole number of bags can be sold because a bag cannot be opened up and divided into fractional parts, then we need to be more precise about our restriction on x. Specifically, we must say that x is a positive integer, or $x \geq 0$. Now, it is clear that only 0, 1, 2, 3, etc. bags can be sold as opposed to 1.25 bags or 5.7 bags.

- With respect to Table B, the rule that describes this function was $y = 16x^2$. Does this problem require the same restrictions on x as the previous problem? Explain.

  - *We should state that x must be a positive number because x represents the amount of time traveled, but we do not need to say that x must be a positive integer. The intervals of time do not need to be in whole seconds; the distance can be measured at fractional parts of a second.*

- We describe these different rates as discrete and continuous. When only positive integers make sense for the input of a function, like the bags of candy example, we say that it is a discrete rate problem. When there are no gaps in the values of the input, for example fractional values of time, we say that it is a continuous rate problem. In terms of functions, we see the difference reflected in the input values of the function. We cannot do problems of motion using the concept of unit rate without discussing the meaning of constant speed.

> **Scaffolding:**
> The definition of *discrete* is individually separate or distinct. Knowing this can help students understand why we call certain rates discrete rates.

Example 1 (6 minutes)

This is another example of a discrete rate problem.

Example 1

If 4 copies of the same book cost $256, what is the unit rate for the book?

The unit rate is $\dfrac{256}{4}$ or 64 dollars per book.

- The total cost is a function of the number of books that are purchased. That is, if x is the cost of a book and y is the total cost, then $y = 64x$.

- What cost does the function assign to 3 books? 3.5 books?

  - *For 3 books: $y = 64(3)$, the cost of 3 books is $192.*
  - *For 3.5 books: $y = 64(3.5)$, the cost of 3.5 books is $224.*

- We can use the rule that describes the cost function to determine the cost of 3.5 books, but does it make sense?

  - *No, you cannot buy half of a book.*

- Is this a discrete rate problem or a continuous rate problem? Explain.

  - *This is a discrete rate problem because you cannot buy a fraction of a book; only a whole number of books can be purchased.*

Example 2 (2 minutes)

This is an example of a continuous rate problem examined in the last lesson.

- Let's revisit a problem that we examined in the last lesson.

Example 2

Water flows from a faucet at a constant rate. That is, the volume of water that flows out of the faucet is the same over any given time interval. If 7 gallons of water flow from the faucet every 2 minutes, determine the rule that describes the volume function of the faucet.

- We said then that the rule that describes the volume function of the faucet is $y = 3.5x$, where y is the volume of water in gallons that flows from the faucet and x is the number of minutes the faucet is on.
- What limitations are there on x and y?
  - *Both x and y should be positive numbers because they represent time and volume.*
- Would this rate be considered discrete or continuous? Explain.
  - *This rate is continuous because we can assign a number to any positive value of x, not just integers.*

Example 3 (8 minutes)

This is a more complicated example of a continuous rate problem.

Example 3

You have just been served freshly made soup that is so hot that it cannot be eaten. You measure the temperature of the soup, and it is 210°F. Since 212°F is boiling, there is no way it can safely be eaten yet. One minute after receiving the soup the temperature has dropped to 203°F. If you assume that the rate at which the soup cools is linear, write a rule that would describe the rate of cooling of the soup.

The temperature of the soup dropped 7°F in one minute. Assuming the cooling continues at the same rate, then if y is the number of degrees that the soup drops after x minutes pass, $y = 7x$.

Scaffolding:

The more real you can make this, the better. Consider having a cooling cup of soup, coffee, or tea with a digital thermometer available for students to observe.

- We want to know how long it will be before the temperature of the soup is at a more tolerable temperature of 147°F.   The difference in temperature from 210°F to 147°F is 63°F. For what number x will our function assign 63?
  - $63 = 7x$, *then $x = 9$. Our function assigns 63 to 9.*
- Recall that we assumed that the cooling of the soup would be linear. However, that assumption appears to be incorrect. The data in the table below shows a much different picture of the cooling soup.

time	temperature
after 2 minutes	196
after 3 minutes	190
after 4 minutes	184
after 5 minutes	178
after 6 minutes	173
after 7 minutes	168
after 8 minutes	163
after 9 minutes	158

Our function led us to believe that after 9 minutes the soup would be safe to eat. The data in the table shows that it is still too hot!

- What do you notice about the change in temperature from one minute to the next?
  - *For the first few minutes, minute 2 to minute 5, the temperature decreased 6°F each minute. From minute 5 to minute 9, the temperature decreased just 5°F each minute.*

- Since the rate of cooling at each minute is not linear, then this function is said to be a non-linear function. In fact, the rule that describes the cooling of the soup is

$$y = 70 + 140 \left(\frac{133}{140}\right)^x,$$

where y is the temperature of the soup after x minutes.

- Finding a rule that describes a function like this one is something you will spend more time on in high school. In this module, the non-linear functions we work with will be much simpler. The point is that non-linear functions exist, and in some cases, we cannot think of mathematics as computations of simple numbers. In fact, some functions cannot be described with numbers at all!

- Would this function be described as discrete or continuous? Explain?

  □ *This function is continuous because we could find the temperature of the soup for any fractional time x, as opposed to just integer intervals of time.*

Example 4 (6 minutes)

Example 4

Consider the following function: There is a function G so that the function assigns to each input, the number of a particular player, an output, their height. For example, the function G assigns to the input, 1 an output of 5'11".

1	5'11"
2	5'4"
3	5'9"
4	5'6"
5	6'3"
6	6'8"
7	5'9"
8	5'10"
9	6'2"

- The function G assigns to the input 2 what output?

  □ *The function G would assign the height 5'4" to the player 2.*

- Could the function G also assign to the player 2 a second output value of 5'6"? Explain.

  □ *No. The function assigns height to a particular player. There is no way that a player can have two different heights.*

- Can you think of a way to describe this function using a rule? Of course not. There is no formula for such a function. The only way to describe the function would be to list the assignments shown in part in the table.

- Can we classify this function as discrete or continuous? Explain.

  □ *This function would be described as discrete because the input is a particular player and the output is their height. A person is one height or another, not two heights at the same time.*

- This function is an example of a function that cannot be described by numbers or symbols, but it is still a function.

Exercises 1–3 (10 minutes)

Exercises 1–3

1. A linear function has the table of values below related to the number of buses needed for a fieldtrip.

Number of students (x)	35	70	105	140
Number of buses (y)	1	2	3	4

   a. Write the linear function that represents the number of buses needed, y, for x number of students.

$$y = \frac{1}{35}x$$

   b. Describe the limitations of x and y.

   Both x and y must be positive whole numbers. The symbol x represents students, so we cannot have 1.2 students. Similarly, y represents the number of buses needed, so we cannot have a fractional number of buses.

   c. Is the rate discrete or continuous?

   The rate is discrete.

   d. The entire 8th grade student body of 321 students is going on a fieldtrip. What number of buses does our function assign to 321 students? Explain.

$$y = \frac{1}{35}(321)$$
$$y = \frac{321}{35}$$
$$y = 9.1714\ldots$$
$$y \approx 9.2$$

   Ten buses will be needed for the field trip. The function gives us an assignment of about 9.2, which means that 9.2 buses would be needed for the field trip, but we need a whole number of buses. Nine buses means some students will be left behind, so 10 buses will be needed to take all 321 students on the trip.

   e. Some 7th grade students are going on their own field trip to a different destination, but just 180 are attending. What number does the function assign to 180? How many buses will be needed for the trip?

$$y = \frac{1}{35}(180)$$
$$y = 5.1428\ldots$$
$$y \approx 5.1$$

   Six buses will be needed for the field trip.

   f. What number does the function assign to 50? Explain what this means and what your answer means.

$$y = \frac{1}{35}(50)$$
$$y = 1.4285\ldots$$
$$y \approx 1.4$$

   The question is asking us to determine the number of buses needed for 50 students. The function assigns, approximately 1.4 to 50. The function tells us that we need 1.4 buses for 50 students, but it makes more sense to say we need 2 buses because you cannot have 1.4 buses.

2. A linear function has the table of values below related to the cost of movie tickets.

Number of tickets (x)	3	6	9	12
Total cost (y)	$27.75	$55.50	$83.25	$111

a. Write the linear function that represents the total cost, y, for x tickets purchased.

$$y = \frac{27.75}{3}x$$
$$y = 9.25x$$

b. Is the rate discrete or continuous? Explain.

The rate is discrete. You cannot have half of a movie ticket; therefore, it must be a whole number of tickets which means it is discrete.

c. What number does the function assign to 4? What does the question and your answer mean?

It is asking us to determine the cost of buying 4 tickets. The function assigns 37 to 4. The answers means that four tickets will cost $37.00.

3. A function produces the following table of values.

Input	Output
Banana	Yellow
Cherry	Red
Orange	Orange
Tangerine	Orange
Strawberry	Red

a. Can this function be described by a rule using numbers? Explain.

No, much like the example with the players and their heights, this function cannot be described by numbers or a rule. There is no number or rule that can define the function.

b. Describe the assignment of the function.

The function assigns to each fruit the color of its skin.

c. State an input and the assignment the function would give to its output.

Answers will vary. Accept an answer that satisfies the function; for example, the function would assign red to the input of tomato.

Closing (4 minutes)

Summarize, or ask students to summarize, the main points from the lesson:

- We know that not all functions are linear and, moreover, not all functions can be described by numbers.
- We know that linear functions can have discrete rates and continuous rates.
- We know that discrete rates are those where only integer inputs can be used in the function for the inputs to make sense. An example of this would be purchasing 3 books compared to 3.5 books.
- We know that continuous rates are those where we can use any interval, including fractional values, as an input. An example of this would be determining the distance traveled after 2.5 minutes of walking.

Lesson Summary

Not all functions are linear. In fact, not all functions can be described using numbers.

Linear functions can have discrete rates and continuous rates.

A rate that can have only integer inputs may be used in a function so that it makes sense, and it is then called a <u>discrete rate</u>. For example, when planning for a field trip, it only makes sense to plan for a whole number of students and a whole number of buses, not fractional values of either.

<u>Continuous rates</u> are those where any interval, including fractional values, can be used for an input. For example, determining the distance a person walks for a given time interval. The input, which is time in this case, can be in minutes or fractions of minutes.

Exit Ticket (4 minutes)

Name _____   Date _____

Lesson 4: More Examples of Functions

Exit Ticket

1. A linear function has the table of values below related to the cost of a certain tablet.

Number of tablets (x)	17	22	25
Total cost (y)	$10,183	$13,178	$14,975

    a. Write the linear function that represents the total cost, y, for x number of tablets.

    b. Is the rate discrete or continuous? Explain.

    c. What number does the function assign to 7? Explain.

2. A function produces the following table of values.

Serious	Adjective
Student	Noun
Work	Verb
They	Pronoun
And	Conjunction
Accurately	Adverb

    a. Describe the function.

    b. What part of speech would the function assign to the word continuous?

Exit Ticket Sample Solutions

1. A linear function has the table of values below related to the cost of a certain tablet.

Number of tablets (x)	17	22	25
Total cost (y)	$10,183	$13,178	$14,975

  a. Write the linear function that represents the total cost, y, for x number of tablets.

$$y = \frac{10,183}{17}x$$
$$y = 599x$$

  b. Is the rate discrete or continuous? Explain.

  The rate is discrete. You cannot have half of a tablet; therefore, it must be a whole number of tablets which means it is discrete.

  c. What number does the function assign to 7? Explain.

  The function assigns $4,193$ to 7, which means that the cost of 7 tablets would be $4,193.00.

2. A function produces the following table of values.

Serious	Adjective
Student	Noun
Work	Verb
They	Pronoun
And	Conjunction
Accurately	Adverb

  a. Describe the function.

  The function assigns to each input, a word, the parts of speech.

  b. What part of speech would the function assign to the word continuous?

  The function would assign the word adjective to the word continuous.

Problem Set Sample Solutions

1. A linear function has the table of values below related to the total cost for gallons of gas purchased.

Number of gallons (x)	5.4	6	15	17
Total cost (y)	$19.71	$21.90	$54.75	$62.05

a. Write the linear function that represents the total cost, y, for x gallons of gas.

$$y = 3.65x$$

b. Describe the limitations of x and y.

Both x and y must be positive rational numbers.

c. Is the rate discrete or continuous?

The rate is continuous.

d. What number does the function assign to 20? Explain what your answer means.

$$y = 3.65(20)$$
$$y = 73$$

The function assigns 73 to 20. It means that if 20 gallons of gas are purchased, it will cost $73.

2. A function has the table of values below. Examine the information in the table to answer the questions below.

Input	Output
one	3
two	3
three	5
four	4
five	4
six	3
seven	5

a. Describe the function.

The function assigns to each input, a word, the number of letters in the word.

b. What number would the function assign to the word "eleven"?

The function would assign the number 6 to the word eleven.

3.   A linear function has the table of values below related to the total number of miles driven in a given time interval in hours.

Number of hours driven (x)	3	4	5	6
Total miles driven (y)	141	188	235	282

a.   Write the linear function that represents the total miles driven, y, for x number of hours.

$$y = \frac{141}{3}x$$
$$y = 47x$$

b.   Describe the limitations of x and y.

Both x and y must be positive rational numbers.

c.   Is the rate discrete or continuous?

The rate is continuous.

d.   What number does the function assign to 8? Explain what your answer means.

$$y = 47(8)$$
$$y = 376$$

The function assigns 376 to 8. The answer means that 376 miles are driven in 8 hours.

e.   Use the function to determine how much time it would take to drive 500 miles.

$$500 = 47x$$
$$\frac{500}{47} = x$$
$$10.63829\ldots = x$$
$$10.6 \approx x$$

It would take about 10.6 hours to drive 500 miles.

4.   A function has the table of values below that gives temperatures at specific times over a period of 8 hours.

12:00 p.m.	92°
1:00 p.m.	90.5°
2:00 p.m.	89°
4:00 p.m.	86°
8:00 p.m.	80°

a.   Is the function a linear function? Explain.

Yes, it is a linear function. The change in temperature is the same over each time interval. For example, the temperature drops $1.5°$ from 12:00–1:00 and 1:00–2:00. The temperature drops $3°$ from 2:00–4:00, which is the same as $1.5°$ each hour and $6°$ over a four hour period of time, which is also $1.5°$ per hour.

b.   **Describe the limitations of x and y.**

The input is a particular time of the day and y is the temperature. The input cannot be negative, but could be intervals that are fractions of an hour. The output could potentially be negative because it can get that cold.

c.   **Is the rate discrete or continuous?**

The rate is continuous. The input can be any interval of time, including fractional amounts.

d.   **Let y represent the temperature and x represent the number of hours from 12:00 p.m. Write a rule that describes the function of time on temperature.**

$$y = 92 - 1.5x$$

e.   **Check that the rule you wrote to describe the function works for each of the input and output values given in the table.**

At 12:00, 0 hours have passed since 12:00, then $y = 92 - 1.5(0) = 92$.

At 1:00, 1 hour has passed since 12:00, then $y = 92 - 1.5(1) = 90.5$.

At 2:00, 2 hours have passed since 12:00, then $y = 92 - 1.5(2) = 89$.

At 4:00, 4 hours have passed since 12:00, then $y = 92 - 1.5(4) = 86$.

At 8:00, 8 hours have passed since 12:00, then $y = 92 - 1.5(8) = 80$.

f.   **Use the function to determine the temperature at 5:30 pm.**

At 5:30, 5.5 hours have passed since 12:00, then $y = 92 - 1.5(5.5) = 83.75$.

The temperature at 5:30 will be $83.75°$.

g.   **Is it reasonable to assume that this function could be used to predict the temperature for 10:00 a.m. the following day or a temperature at any time on a day next week? Give specific examples in your explanation.**

No, the function can only predict the temperature for as long as the temperature is decreasing. At some point the temperature will rise. For example, if we tried to predict the temperature for a week from 12:00 p.m. when the data was first collected, we would have to use the function to determine what number it assigns to 168 because 168 would be the number of hours that pass in the week. Then we would have

$$y = 92 - 1.5(168)$$
$$y = -160$$

which is an unreasonable prediction for the temperature.

Lesson 5: Graphs of Functions and Equations

Student Outcomes

- Students know that the definition of a graph of a function is the set of ordered pairs consisting of an input and the corresponding output.
- Students understand why the graph of a function is identical to the graph of a certain equation.

Classwork

Exploratory Challenge/Exercises 1–3 (15 minutes)

Students work independently or in pairs to complete Exercises 1-3

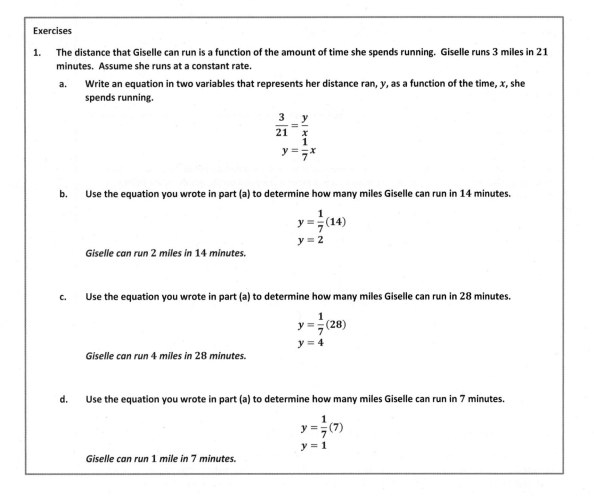

Exercises

1. The distance that Giselle can run is a function of the amount of time she spends running. Giselle runs 3 miles in 21 minutes. Assume she runs at a constant rate.

    a. Write an equation in two variables that represents her distance ran, y, as a function of the time, x, she spends running.

$$\frac{3}{21} = \frac{y}{x}$$
$$y = \frac{1}{7}x$$

    b. Use the equation you wrote in part (a) to determine how many miles Giselle can run in 14 minutes.

$$y = \frac{1}{7}(14)$$
$$y = 2$$

    Giselle can run 2 miles in 14 minutes.

    c. Use the equation you wrote in part (a) to determine how many miles Giselle can run in 28 minutes.

$$y = \frac{1}{7}(28)$$
$$y = 4$$

    Giselle can run 4 miles in 28 minutes.

    d. Use the equation you wrote in part (a) to determine how many miles Giselle can run in 7 minutes.

$$y = \frac{1}{7}(7)$$
$$y = 1$$

    Giselle can run 1 mile in 7 minutes.

e.   The input of the function, x, is time and the output of the function, y, is the distance Giselle ran. Write the input and outputs from parts (b)–(d) as ordered pairs and plot them as points on a coordinate plane.

$$(14, 2), (28, 4), (7, 1)$$

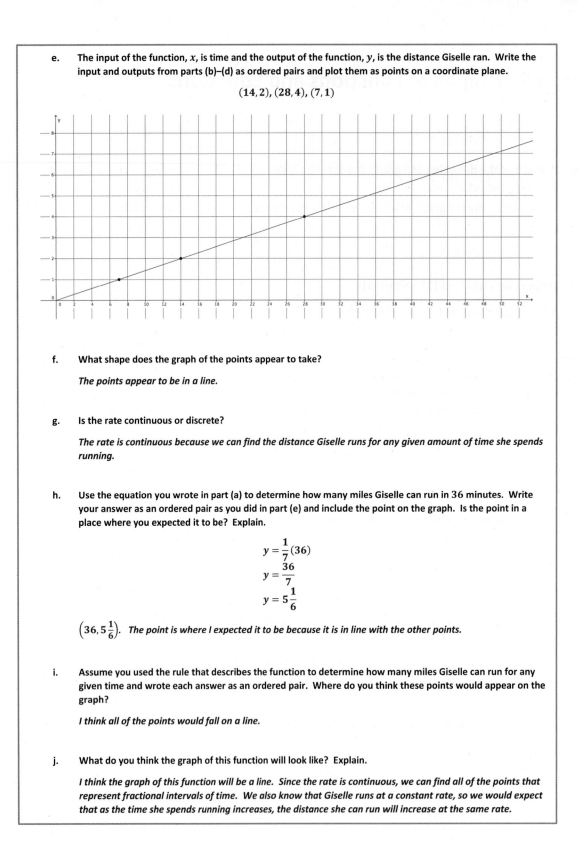

f.   What shape does the graph of the points appear to take?

The points appear to be in a line.

g.   Is the rate continuous or discrete?

The rate is continuous because we can find the distance Giselle runs for any given amount of time she spends running.

h.   Use the equation you wrote in part (a) to determine how many miles Giselle can run in 36 minutes. Write your answer as an ordered pair as you did in part (e) and include the point on the graph. Is the point in a place where you expected it to be? Explain.

$$y = \frac{1}{7}(36)$$
$$y = \frac{36}{7}$$
$$y = 5\frac{1}{6}$$

$\left(36, 5\frac{1}{6}\right)$. *The point is where I expected it to be because it is in line with the other points.*

i.   Assume you used the rule that describes the function to determine how many miles Giselle can run for any given time and wrote each answer as an ordered pair. Where do you think these points would appear on the graph?

I think all of the points would fall on a line.

j.   What do you think the graph of this function will look like? Explain.

I think the graph of this function will be a line. Since the rate is continuous, we can find all of the points that represent fractional intervals of time. We also know that Giselle runs at a constant rate, so we would expect that as the time she spends running increases, the distance she can run will increase at the same rate.

k. Connect the points you have graphed to make a line. Select a point on the graph that has integer coordinates. Verify that this point has an output that the function would assign to the input.

Answers will vary. Sample student work:

The point $(42, 6)$ is a point on the graph.

$$y = \frac{1}{7}x$$
$$6 = \frac{1}{7}(42)$$
$$6 = 6$$

The function assigns the output of 6 to the input of 42.

l. Graph the equation $y = \frac{1}{7}x$ using the same coordinate plane in part (e). What do you notice about the graph of the function that describes Giselle's constant rate of running and the graph of the equation $y = \frac{1}{7}x$?

The graphs of the equation and the function coincide completely.

2. Graph the equation $y = x^2$ for positive values of x. Organize your work using the table below, and then answer the questions that follow.

x	y
0	0
1	1
2	4
3	9
4	16
5	25
6	36

a. Graph the ordered pairs on the coordinate plane.

b. What shape does the graph of the points appear to take?

It appears to take the shape of a curve.

c. Is this equation a linear equation? Explain.

No, the equation $y = x^2$ is not a linear equation because the exponent of x is greater than 1.

d. An area function has the rule so that it assigns to each input, the length of one side of a square, s, an output, the area of the square, A. Write the rule for this function.

$$A = s^2$$

e. What do you think the graph of this function will look like? Explain.

I think the graph of this function will look like the graph of the equation $y = x^2$. The inputs and outputs would match the solutions to the equation exactly. For the equation, the y value is the square of x value. For the function, the output is the square of the input.

f.   Use the function you wrote in part (d) to determine the area of a square with side length 2.5. Write the input and output as an ordered pair. Does this point appear to belong to the graph of $y = x^2$?

$$A = (2.5)^2$$
$$A = 6.25$$

$(2.5, 6.25)$ *The point looks like it would belong to the graph of $y = x^2$, it looks like it would be on the curve that the shape of the graph is taking.*

3.   The number of devices a particular manufacturing company can produce is a function of the number of hours spent making the devices. On average, 4 devices are produced each hour. Assume that devices are produced at a constant rate.

a.   Write an equation in two variables that represents the number of devices, y, as a function of the time the company spends making the devices, x.

$$\frac{4}{1} = \frac{y}{x}$$
$$y = 4x$$

b.   Use the equation you wrote in part (a) to determine how many devices are produced in 8 hours.

$$y = 4(8)$$
$$y = 32$$

The company produces 32 devices in 8 hours.

c.   Use the equation you wrote in part (a) to determine how many devices are produced in 6 hours.

$$y = 4(6)$$
$$y = 24$$

The company produces 24 devices in 6 hours.

d.   Use the equation you wrote in part (a) to determine how many devices are produced in 4 hours.

$$y = 4(4)$$
$$y = 16$$

The company produces 16 devices in 4 hours.

e.   The input of the function, x, is time and the output of the function, y, is the number of devices produced. Write the input and outputs from parts (b)–(d) as ordered pairs and plot them as points on a coordinate plane.

$(8, 32), (6, 24), (4, 16)$

f.   What shape does the graph of the points appear to take?

The points appear to be in a line.

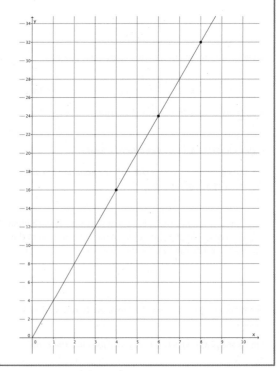

g.   Is the rate continuous or discrete?

The rate is continuous because we can find the number of devices produced for any given time, including fractions of an hour.

h.   Use the equation you wrote in part (a) to determine how many devices are produced in 1.5 hours. Write your answer as an ordered pair as you did in part (e) and include the point on the graph. Is the point in a place where you expected it to be? Explain.

$$y = 4(1.5)$$
$$y = 6$$

$(1.5, 6)$. *The point is where I expected it to be because it is in line with the other points.*

i.   Assume you used the rule that describes the function to determine how many devices are produced for any given time and wrote each answer as an ordered pair. Where do you think these points would appear on the graph?

I think all of the points would fall on a line.

j.   What do you think the graph of this function will look like? Explain.

I think the graph of this function will be a line. Since the rate is continuous, we can find all of the points that represent fractional intervals of time. We also know that devices are produced at a constant rate, so we would expect that as the time spent producing devices increases, the number of devices produced would increase at the same rate.

k.   Connect the points you have graphed to make a line. Select a point on the graph that has integer coordinates. Verify that this point has an output that the function would assign to the input.

Answers will vary. Sample student work:

The point $(5, 20)$ is a point on the graph.

$$y = 4x$$
$$20 = 4(5)$$
$$20 = 20$$

The function assigns the output of 20 to the input of 5.

l.   Graph the equation $y = 4x$ using the same coordinate plane in part (e). What do you notice about the graph of the function that describes the company's constant rate of producing devices and the graph of the equation $y = 4x$?

The graphs of the equation and the function coincide completely.

Discussion (10 minutes)

▪   What was the rule that described the function in Exercise 1?

□   *The rule was $y = \frac{1}{7}x$.*

▪   Given an input, how did you determine the output that the function would assign?

□   *We used the rule. In place of x, we put the input. The number that was computed was the output.*

MP.6

- When you wrote your inputs and corresponding outputs as ordered pairs, what you were doing can be described generally by the ordered pair $\left(x, \frac{1}{7}x\right)$.

Give students a moment to make sense of the ordered pair and verify that it matches their work in Exercise 1. Then continue with the discussion.

- When we first began graphing linear equations in two variables, we used a table and picked a value for x and then used that x to compute the value of y. For an equation of the form $y = \frac{1}{7}x$, the ordered pairs that represent solutions to the equation can be described generally by $\left(x, \frac{1}{7}x\right)$.

- How does the ordered pair from the function compare to the ordered pair of the equation?
  - *The ordered pairs of the function and the equation are exactly the same.*

- What does that mean about the graph of a function compared to the graph of an equation?
  - *It means the graph of a function will be the same as the graph of the equation.*

- Can we make similar conclusions about Exercise 2?

Give students time to verify that the conclusions about Exercise 2 are the same as the conclusions about Exercise 1. Then continue with the discussion.

- What ordered pair generally describes the inputs and corresponding outputs of Exercise 2?
  - $(x, 4x)$.

- What ordered pair generally describes the x and y values of the equation $y = 4x$?
  - $(x, 4x)$.

- What does that mean about the graph of the function and the graph of the equation?
  - *It means that the graph of the function is the same as the graph of the equation.*

- For Exercise 3, you began by graphing the equation $y = x^2$ for positive values of x. What was the shape of the graph?
  - *It looked curved.*

- The graph had a curve in it because it was not the graph of a linear equation. All linear equations graph as lines. That is what we learned in Module 4. Since this equation was not linear, we should expect it to graph as something other than a line.

- What did you notice about the ordered pairs of the equation $y = x^2$ and the inputs and corresponding outputs for the function $A = s^2$?
  - *The ordered pairs were exactly the same for the equation and the function.*

- What does that mean about the graphs of functions, even those that are not linear?
  - *It means that the graph of a function will be identical to the graph of an equation.*

- Now we know that we can graph linear and non-linear functions by writing their inputs and corresponding outputs as ordered pairs. The graphs of functions will be the same as the graphs of the equations that describe them.

Exploratory Challenge/Exercise 4 (7 minutes)

Students work in pairs to complete Exercise 4.

4. Examine the three graphs below. Which, if any, could represent the graph of a function? Explain why or why not for each graph.

    Graph 1:

    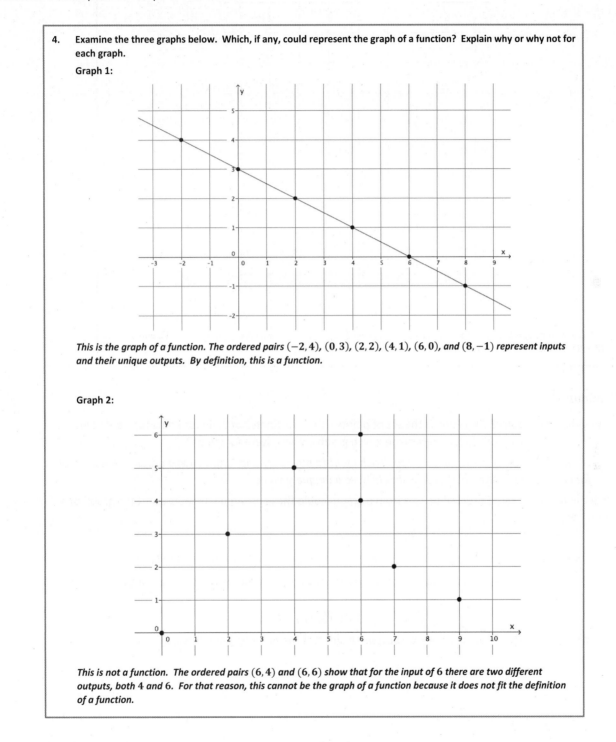

    This is the graph of a function. The ordered pairs $(-2, 4)$, $(0, 3)$, $(2, 2)$, $(4, 1)$, $(6, 0)$, and $(8, -1)$ represent inputs and their unique outputs. By definition, this is a function.

    Graph 2:

    This is not a function. The ordered pairs $(6, 4)$ and $(6, 6)$ show that for the input of 6 there are two different outputs, both 4 and 6. For that reason, this cannot be the graph of a function because it does not fit the definition of a function.

Graph 3:

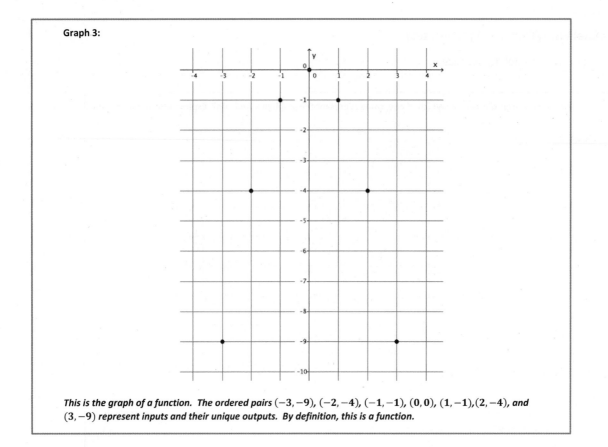

This is the graph of a function. The ordered pairs $(-3, -9)$, $(-2, -4)$, $(-1, -1)$, $(0, 0)$, $(1, -1)$, $(2, -4)$, *and* $(3, -9)$ *represent inputs and their unique outputs. By definition, this is a function.*

Discussion (3 minutes)

- We know that the graph of a function is the set of points with coordinates of an input and a corresponding output. How did you use this fact to determine which graphs, if any, were functions?

  □ *By the definition of a function, we need each input to have only one output. On a graph, it means that for each of the ordered pairs, the x should have a unique y value.*

- Assume the following set of ordered pairs is from a graph, could these ordered pairs represent the graph of a function? Explain.

$$(3, 5), (4, 7), (3, 9), (5, -2)$$

  □ *No because the input of 3 has two different outputs. It does not fit the definition of a function.*

- Assume the following set of ordered pairs is from a graph, could these ordered pairs represent the graph of a function? Explain.

$$(-1, 6), (-3, 8), (5, 10), (7, 6)$$

  □ *Yes because each input has a unique output. It satisfies the definition of a function.*

▪ Which of the following four graphs are functions? Explain.

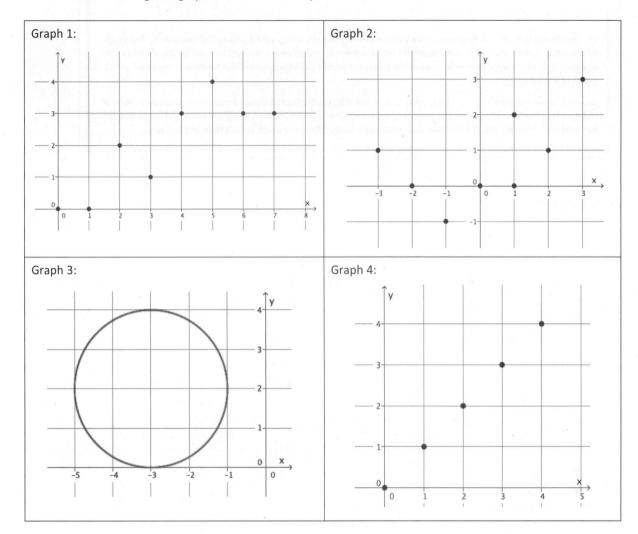

Graph 1:

Graph 2:

Graph 3:

Graph 4:

▫ *Graphs 1 and 4 are functions. Graphs 2 and 3 are not. Graphs 1 and 4 show that for each input of x, there is a unique output of y. For Graph 2, the input of $x = 1$ has two different outputs, $y = 0$ and $y = 2$, which means it cannot be a function. For Graph 3, It appears that each value of x has two outputs, one on the lower half of the circle and one on the upper half, which means it does not fit the definition of function.*

Closing (5 minutes)

Summarize, or ask students to summarize, the main points from the lesson:

▪ We know that we can graph a function by writing the inputs and corresponding outputs as ordered pairs.

▪ We know that the graph of a function is the same as the graph of the rule (equation) that describes it.

▪ We know that we can examine a graph to determine if it is the graph of a function, specifically to make sure that each value of x (inputs) has only one y value (outputs).

Lesson Summary

The inputs and outputs of a function can be written as ordered pairs and graphed on a coordinate plane. The graph of a function is the same as the rule (equation) that describes it. For example, if a function can be described by the equation $y = mx$, then the ordered pairs of the graph are (x, mx) and the graph of the function is the same as the graph of the equation, $y = mx$.

One way to determine if a set of data is a function or not is by examining the inputs and outputs given by a table. If the data is in the form of a graph, the process is the same. That is, examine each coordinate of x and verify that it has only one y coordinate. If each input has exactly one output, then the graph is the graph of a function.

Exit Ticket (5 minutes)

Name _____   Date _____

Lesson 5: Graphs of Functions and Equations

Exit Ticket

1.   The amount of water in gallons that flows out a certain hose is a function of the amount of time the faucet is turned on. The amount of water that flows out of the hose in four minutes is eleven gallons. Assume water flows at a constant rate.

     a.   Write an equation in two variables that represents the amount in gallons of water, y, as a function of the time, x, the faucet is turned on.

     b.   Use the equation you wrote in part (a) to determine the amount of water that flows out of a hose in 8 minutes, 4 minutes, and 2 minutes.

     c.   The input of the function, x, is time and the output of the function, y, is the amount of water that flows out of the hose in gallons. Write the input and outputs from part (b) as ordered pairs and plot them as points on a coordinate plane.

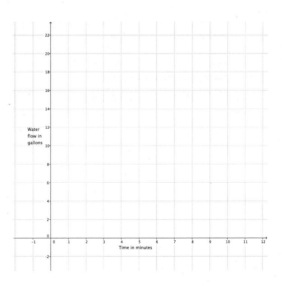

Exit Ticket Sample Solutions

1. The amount of water in gallons that flows out a certain hose is a function of the amount of time the faucet is turned on. The amount of water that flows out of the hose in four minutes is eleven gallons. Assume water flows at a constant rate.

    a. Write an equation in two variables that represents the amount in gallons of water, y, as a function of the time, x, the faucet is turned on.

    $$\frac{11}{4} = \frac{y}{x}$$
    $$y = \frac{11}{4}x$$

    b. Use the equation you wrote in part (a) to determine the amount of water that flows out of a hose in 8 minutes, 4 minutes, and 2 minutes.

    $$y = \frac{11}{4}(8)$$
    $$y = 22$$

    In 8 minutes, 22 gallons of water flow out of the hose.

    $$y = \frac{11}{4}(4)$$
    $$y = 11$$

    In 4 minutes, 11 gallons of water flows out of the hose.

    $$y = \frac{11}{4}(2)$$
    $$y = 5.5$$

    In 2 minutes, 5.5 gallons of water flow out of the hose.

    c. The input of the function, x, is time and the output of the function, y, is the amount of water that flows out of the hose in gallons. Write the input and outputs from part (b) as ordered pairs, and plot them as points on a coordinate plane.

    $(8, 22), (4, 11), (2, 5.5)$

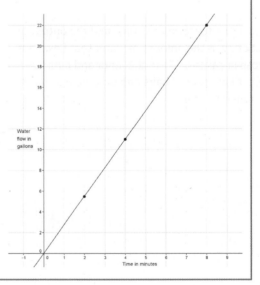

Problem Set Sample Solutions

1. The distance that Scott walks is a function of the time he spends walking. Scott can walk $\frac{1}{2}$ mile every 8 minutes. Assume he walks at a constant rate.

    a. Predict the shape of the graph of the function. Explain.

        The graph of the function will likely be a line because a linear equation can describe Scott's motion, and I know that the graph of the function will be the same as the graph of the equation.

    b. Write an equation to represent the distance that Scott can walk, y, in x minutes.

$$\frac{0.5}{8} = \frac{y}{x}$$
$$y = \frac{0.5}{8}x$$
$$y = \frac{1}{16}x$$

    c. Use the equation you wrote in part (b) to determine how many miles Scott can walk in 24 minutes.

$$y = \frac{1}{16}(24)$$
$$y = 1.5$$

    Scott can walk 1.5 miles in 24 minutes.

    d. Use the equation you wrote in part (a) to determine how many miles Scott can walk in 12 minutes.

$$y = \frac{1}{16}(12)$$
$$y = \frac{3}{4}$$

    Scott can walk 0.75 miles in 12 minutes.

    e. Use the equation you wrote in part (a) to determine how many miles Scott can walk in 16 minutes.

$$y = \frac{1}{16}(16)$$
$$y = 1$$

    Scott can walk 1 mile in 16 minutes.

f.   Write your inputs and corresponding outputs as ordered pairs. Then graph them on a coordinate plane.

$(24, 1.5), (12, 0.75), (16, 1)$

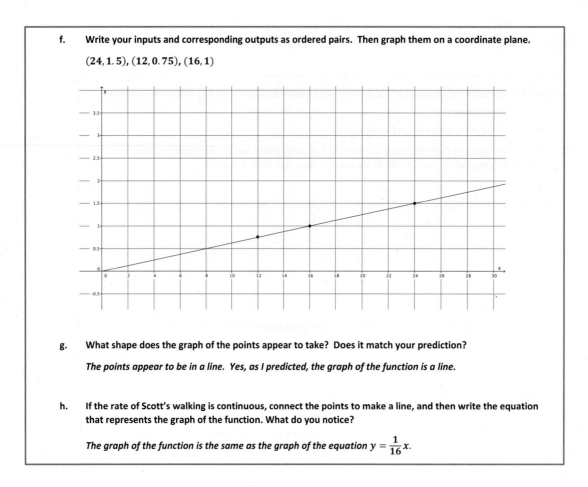

g.   What shape does the graph of the points appear to take? Does it match your prediction?

The points appear to be in a line. Yes, as I predicted, the graph of the function is a line.

h.   If the rate of Scott's walking is continuous, connect the points to make a line, and then write the equation that represents the graph of the function. What do you notice?

The graph of the function is the same as the graph of the equation $y = \frac{1}{16}x$.

2. Graph the equation $y = x^3$ for positive values of x. Organize your work using the table below, and then answer the questions that follow.

x	y
0	0
0.5	0.125
1	1
1.5	3.375
2	8
2.5	15.625

a. Graph the ordered pairs on the coordinate plane.

b. What shape does the graph of the points appear to take?

It appears to take the shape of a curve.

c. Is this the graph of a linear function? Explain.

No, this is not the graph of a linear function. The equation $y = x^3$ is not a linear equation because the exponent of x is greater than 1.

d. A volume function has the rule so that it assigns to each input, the length of one side of a cube, s, the output, the volume of the cube, V. The rule for this function is $V = s^3$. What do you think the graph of this function will look like? Explain.

I think the graph of this function will look like the graph of the equation $y = x^3$. The inputs and outputs would match the solutions to the equation exactly. For the equation, the y value is the cube of x value. For the function, the output is the cube of the input.

e. Use the function in part (d) to determine the area of a volume with side length of 3. Write the input and output as an ordered pair. Does this point appear to belong to the graph of $y = x^3$?

$$A = (3)^3$$
$$A = 27$$

$(3, 27)$ *The point looks like it would belong to the graph of $y = x^3$, it looks like it would be on the curve that the shape of the graph is taking.*

EUREKA
MATH™

3. Graph the equation $y = 180(x - 2)$ for whole numbers. Organize your work using the table below, and then answer the questions that follow.

x	y
3	180
4	360
5	540
6	720

a. Graph the ordered pairs on the coordinate plane.

b. What shape does the graph of the points appear to take?

   It appears to take the shape of a line.

c. Is this graph a graph of a function? How do you know?

   It appears to be a function because each input has exactly one output.

d. Is this a linear equation? Explain.

   Yes, $y = 180(x - 2)$ is a linear equation because the exponent of x is 1.

e. The sum of interior angles of a polygon has the rule so that it assigns each input, the number of sides, n, of the polygon the output, S, the sum of the interior angles of the polygon. The rule for this function is $S = 180(n - 2)$. What do you think the graph of this function will look like? Explain.

   I think the graph of this function will look like the graph of the equation $y = 180(x - 2)$. The inputs and outputs would match the solutions to the equation exactly.

f. Is this function continuous or discrete? Explain.

   The function $S = 180(n - 2)$ is discrete. The inputs are the number of sides, which are integers. The input, n, must be greater than 2 since three sides is the smallest number of sides for a polygon.

4. Examine the graph below. Could the graph represent the graph of a function? Explain why or why not.

   This is not a function. The ordered pairs $(1, 0)$ and $(1, -1)$ show that for the input of 1 there are two different outputs, both 0 and -1. For that reason, this cannot be the graph of a function because it does not fit the definition of a function.

5. Examine the graph below. Could the graph represent the graph of a function? Explain why or why not.

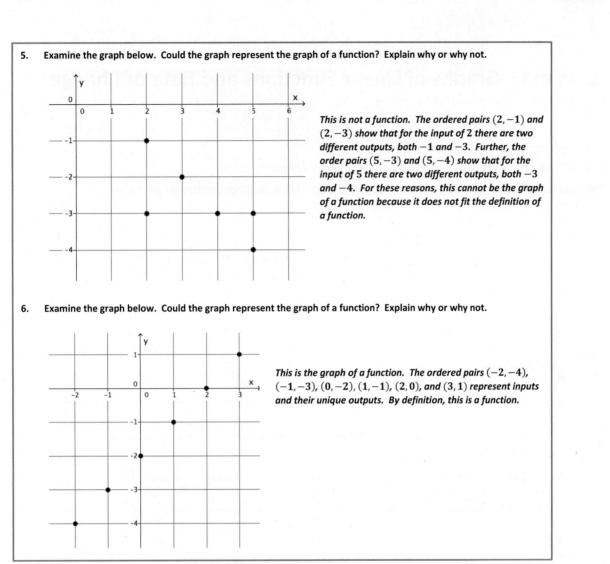

This is not a function. The ordered pairs $(2, -1)$ and $(2, -3)$ show that for the input of 2 there are two different outputs, both -1 and -3. Further, the order pairs $(5, -3)$ and $(5, -4)$ show that for the input of 5 there are two different outputs, both -3 and -4. For these reasons, this cannot be the graph of a function because it does not fit the definition of a function.

6. Examine the graph below. Could the graph represent the graph of a function? Explain why or why not.

This is the graph of a function. The ordered pairs $(-2, -4)$, $(-1, -3)$, $(0, -2)$, $(1, -1)$, $(2, 0)$, and $(3, 1)$ represent inputs and their unique outputs. By definition, this is a function.

Lesson 6: Graphs of Linear Functions and Rate of Change

Student Outcomes

- Students use rate of change to determine if a function is a linear function.
- Students interpret the equation $y = mx + b$ as defining a linear function, whose graph is a line.

Lesson Notes

This lesson contains a fluency exercise that will take approximately 10 minutes. The objective of the fluency exercise is for students to look for and make use of structure while solving multi-step equations. The fluency exercise can occur at any time throughout the lesson.

Classwork

Opening Exercise (5 minutes)

MP.1 & MP.3

Opening Exercise

Functions 1, 2, and 3 have the tables shown below. Examine each of them and make a conjecture about which will be linear and justify your claim.

Input	Output
2	5
4	7
5	8
8	11

Input	Output
2	4
3	9
4	16
5	25

Input	Output
0	−3
1	1
2	6
3	9

Lead a short discussion that allows students to share their conjectures and reasoning. Revisit the Opening Exercise at the end of the discussion so students can verify if their conjectures were correct. Only the first function is a linear function.

Discussion (15 minutes)

Ask students to summarize what they learned from the last lesson. Make sure they note that the graph of a function is the set of ordered pairs of inputs and their corresponding outputs. Also, note that the graph of a function is identical to the graph of the equation or formula that describes it. Next, ask students to recall what they know about rate of change and slope. Finally, ask students to write or share a claim about what they think the graph of a linear function will look like. Tell them that they need to support their claim with some mention of rate of change or slope.

> *Scaffolding:*
> Students may need a brief review of the terms related to linear equations.

- Suppose a function can be described by an equation in the form of $y = mx + b$ and that the function assigns the values shown in the table below:

Input	Output
2	5
3.5	8
4	9
4.5	10

- We want to determine whether or not this is a linear function and if so, we want to determine what the linear equation is that describes the function.

- In Module 4, we learned that linear equations graph as lines and that all lines are graphs of linear equations. Therefore, if we can show that a linear equation produces the same results as the function, then we know that the function is a linear function. How did we compute the slope of the graph of a line?

  □ *To compute slope, we found the difference in y-values compared to the distance in x-values. We used the formula:*

  $$m = \frac{y_1 - y_2}{x_1 - x_2}$$

- Based on what we learned in the last lesson about the graphs of functions (i.e., the input and corresponding output can be expressed as an ordered pair), we can look at the formula as the following:

  $$m = \frac{output_1 - output_2}{input_1 - input_2}$$

  If the rate of change (i.e., slope) is the same for each pair of inputs and outputs, then we know we are looking at a linear function. To that end, we begin with the first two rows of the table:

  $$\frac{5 - 8}{2 - 3.5} = \frac{-3}{-1.5}$$
  $$= 2$$

- Calculate the rate of change between rows two and three and rows three and four.

  □ *Sample student work:*

  $$\frac{8 - 9}{3.5 - 4} = \frac{-1}{-0.5} \qquad\qquad \frac{9 - 10}{4 - 4.5} = \frac{-1}{-0.5}$$
  $$= 2 \qquad\qquad\qquad\qquad = 2$$

- What did you notice?

  □ *The rate of change between each pair of inputs and outputs was 2.*

- To be thorough, we could also look at rows one and three and one and four, there are many combinations to inspect. What will the result be?

  □ *We expect the rate of change to be 2.*

- Verify your claim by checking one more pair.
    - *Sample student work:*

$$\frac{5 - 10}{2 - 4.5} = \frac{5}{-2.5} \qquad \text{or} \qquad \frac{5 - 9}{2 - 4} = \frac{-4}{-2}$$
$$= 2 \qquad\qquad\qquad\qquad = 2$$

- With this knowledge, we have answered the first question because the rate of change is equal to a constant (in this case, 2) between pairs of inputs and their corresponding outputs, then we know that we have a linear function. Next, we find the equation that describes the function. At this point, we expect the equation to be described by $y = 2x + b$ because we know the slope is 2. Since the function assigns 5 to 2, 8 to 3.5, etc., we can use that information to determine the value of b by solving the following equation.

    Using the assignment of 5 to 2:

$$5 = 2(2) + b$$
$$5 = 4 + b$$
$$1 = b$$

- Now that we know that $b = 1$ we can substitute into $y = 2x + b$, which results in the equation $y = 2x + 1$. The equation that describes the function is $y = 2x + 1$ and the function is a linear function. What would the graph of this function look like?
    - *It would be a line because the rule that describes the function in the form of $y = mx + b$ are equations known to graph as lines.*

- The following table represents the outputs that a function would assign to given inputs. We want to know if the function is a linear function, and if so, what linear equation describes the function.

Input	Output
−2	4
3	9
4.5	20.25
5	25

- How should we begin?
    - *We need to inspect the rate of change between pairs of inputs and their corresponding outputs.*

- Compare at least three pairs of inputs and their corresponding outputs.
    - *Sample student work:*

$$\frac{4 - 9}{-2 - 3} = \frac{-5}{-5} \qquad\qquad \frac{4 - 25}{-2 - 5} = \frac{-21}{-7} \qquad\qquad \frac{9 - 25}{3 - 5} = \frac{-16}{-2}$$
$$= 1 \qquad\qquad\qquad = 3 \qquad\qquad\qquad = 8$$

- What do you notice about the rate of change and what does this mean about the function?
    - *The rate of change was different for each pair of inputs and outputs inspected, which means that it is not a linear function.*

- If this were a linear function, what would we expect to see?
    - *If this were a linear function, each inspection of the rate of change would result in the same number (similar to what we saw in the last problem where each result was 2).*

Lesson 6:   Graphs of Linear Functions and Rate of Change

- We have enough evidence to conclude that this function is not a linear function. Would the graph of this function be a line? Explain.

  □ *No, the graph of this function would not be a line. Only linear functions, whose equations are in the form of $y = mx + b$, graph as lines. Since this function does not have a constant rate of change it will not graph as a line.*

Exercise (5 minutes)

Students work independently or in pairs to complete the Exercise.

Exercise

A function assigns the inputs and corresponding outputs shown in the table below.

Input	Output
1	2
2	−1
4	−7
6	−13

a. Is the function a linear function? Check at least three pairs of inputs and their corresponding outputs.

$$\frac{2 - (-1)}{1 - 2} = \frac{3}{-1}$$
$$= -3$$

$$\frac{-7 - (-13)}{4 - 6} = \frac{6}{-2}$$
$$= -3$$

$$\frac{2 - (-7)}{1 - 4} = \frac{9}{-3}$$
$$= -3$$

Yes, the rate of change is the same when I check pairs of inputs and corresponding outputs. Each time it is equal to -3. Since the rate of change is the same, then I know it is a linear function.

b. What equation describes the function?

Using the assignment of 2 to 1:

$$2 = -3(1) + b$$
$$2 = -3 + b$$
$$5 = b$$

The equation that describes the function is $y = -3x + 5$.

c. What will the graph of the function look like? Explain.

The graph of the function will be a line. Since the function is a linear function that can be described by the equation $y = -3x + 5$, then it will graph as a line because equations of the form $y = mx + b$ graph as lines.

Fluency Exercise (10 minutes)

In this exercise students solve three sets of similar multi-step equations. Display the equations one at a time. Each equation should be solved in less than one minute; however, students may need slightly more time for the first set and less time for the next two sets if they notice the pattern. Consider having students work on white boards and have them show you their solutions for each problem. The three sets of equations and their answers are below.

Set 1: Answer for each problem is $x = -2$	Set 2: Answer for each problem is $x = -\dfrac{3}{14}$	Set 3: Answer for each problem is $x = 5$
$3x + 2 = 5x + 6$	$6 - 4x = 10x + 9$	$5x + 2 = 9x - 18$
$4(5x + 6) = 4(3x + 2)$	$-2(-4x + 6) = -2(10x + 9)$	$8x + 2 - 3x = 7x - 18 + 2x$
$\dfrac{3x + 2}{6} = \dfrac{5x + 6}{6}$	$\dfrac{10x + 9}{5} = \dfrac{6 - 4x}{5}$	$\dfrac{2 + 5x}{3} = \dfrac{7x - 18 + 2x}{3}$

Closing (5 minutes)

Summarize, or ask students to summarize, the main points from the lesson:

- We know that if the rate of change for pairs of inputs and corresponding outputs is the same for each pair, the function is a linear function.
- We know that we can write linear equations in the form of $y = mx + b$ to express a linear function.
- We know that the graph of a linear function in the form of $y = mx + b$ will graph as a line because all equations of that form graph as lines. Therefore, if a function can be expressed in the form of $y = mx + b$, the function will graph as a line.

Lesson Summary

When the rate of change is constant for pairs of inputs and their corresponding outputs, the function is a linear function.

We can write linear equations in the form of $y = mx + b$ to express a linear function.

From the last lesson we know that the graph of a function is the same as the graph of the equation that describes it. When a function can be described by the linear equation $y = mx + b$, the graph of the function will be a line because the graph of the equation $y = mx + b$ is a line.

Exit Ticket (5 minutes)

Name _____   Date _____

Lesson 6: Graphs of Linear Functions and Rate of Change

Exit Ticket

1. Sylvie claims that the table of inputs and outputs below will be a linear function. Is she correct? Explain.

Inputs	Outputs
−3	−25
2	10
5	31
8	54

2. A function assigns the inputs and corresponding outputs shown in the table below.

   a. Is the function a linear function? Check at least three pairs of inputs and their corresponding outputs.

Input	Output
−2	3
8	−2
10	−3
20	−8

   b. What equation describes the function?

   c. What will the graph of the function look like? Explain.

Exit Ticket Sample Solutions

1. Sylvie claims that the table of inputs and outputs will be a linear function. Is she correct? Explain.

Inputs	Outputs
−3	−25
2	10
5	31
8	54

$$\frac{-25 - (10)}{-3 - 2} = \frac{-35}{-5}$$
$$= 7$$

$$\frac{10 - 31}{2 - 5} = \frac{-21}{-3}$$
$$= 7$$

$$\frac{31 - 54}{5 - 8} = \frac{-23}{-3}$$
$$= \frac{23}{3}$$

No, this is not a linear function. The rate of change was not the same for each pair of inputs and outputs inspected, which means that it is not a linear function.

2. A function assigns the inputs and corresponding outputs shown in the table below.

   a. Is the function a linear function? Check at least three pairs of inputs and their corresponding outputs.

Input	Output
−2	3
8	−2
10	−3
20	−8

$$\frac{3 - (-2)}{-2 - 8} = \frac{5}{-10} = -\frac{1}{2}$$

$$\frac{-2 - (-3)}{8 - 10} = \frac{1}{-2} = -\frac{1}{2}$$

$$\frac{-3 - (-8)}{10 - 20} = \frac{5}{-10} = -\frac{1}{2}$$

Yes, the rate of change is the same when I check pairs of inputs and corresponding outputs. Each time it is equal to $-\frac{1}{2}$. Since the rate of change is the same, then I know it is a linear function.

   b. What equation describes the function?

   Using the assignment of 3 to − 2:

$$3 = -\frac{1}{2}(-2) + b$$
$$3 = 1 + b$$
$$2 = b$$

   The equation that describes the function is $y = -\frac{1}{2}x + 2$.

   c. What will the graph of the function look like? Explain.

   The graph of the function will be a line. Since the function is a linear function that can be described by the equation $y = -\frac{1}{2}x + 2$, then it will graph as a line because equations of the form $y = mx + b$ graph as lines.

Problem Set Sample Solutions

1. A function assigns the inputs and corresponding outputs shown in the table below.

Input	Output
3	9
9	17
12	21
15	25

a. Is the function a linear function? Check at least three pairs of inputs and their corresponding outputs.

$$\frac{9-17}{3-9} = \frac{-8}{-6} \qquad\qquad \frac{17-21}{9-12} = \frac{-4}{-3} \qquad\qquad \frac{21-25}{12-15} = \frac{-4}{-3}$$

$$= \frac{4}{3} \qquad\qquad\qquad = \frac{4}{3} \qquad\qquad\qquad = \frac{4}{3}$$

Yes, the rate of change is the same when I check pairs of inputs and corresponding outputs. Each time it is equal to $\frac{4}{3}$. Since the rate of change is the same, then I know it is a linear function.

b. What equation describes the function?

Using the assignment of 9 to 3:

$$9 = \frac{4}{3}(3) + b$$
$$9 = 4 + b$$
$$5 = b$$

The equation that describes the function is $y = \frac{4}{3}x + 5$.

c. What will the graph of the function look like? Explain.

The graph of the function will be a line. Since the function is a linear function that can be described by the equation $y = \frac{4}{3}x + 5$, it will graph as a line because equations of the form $y = mx + b$ graph as lines.

2. A function assigns the inputs and corresponding outputs shown in the table below.

Input	Output
−1	2
0	0
1	2
2	8
3	18

a. Is the function a linear function?

$$\frac{2-0}{-1-0} = \frac{2}{-1} \qquad\qquad\qquad \frac{0-2}{0-1} = \frac{-2}{-1}$$

$$= -2 \qquad\qquad\qquad\qquad\qquad = 2$$

No, the rate of change is not the same when I check the first two pairs of inputs and corresponding outputs. All rates of change must be the same for all inputs and outputs for the function to be linear.

b. What equation describes the function?

I am not sure what equation describes the function. It is not a linear function.

3. A function assigns the inputs and corresponding outputs shown in the table below.

Input	Output
0.2	2
0.6	6
1.5	15
2.1	21

a. Is the function a linear function? Check at least three pairs of inputs and their corresponding outputs.

$$\frac{2-6}{0.2-0.6} = \frac{-4}{-0.4} \qquad \frac{6-15}{0.6-1.5} = \frac{-9}{-0.9} \qquad \frac{15-21}{1.5-2.1} = \frac{-6}{-0.6}$$
$$= 10 \qquad\qquad\qquad = 10 \qquad\qquad\qquad = 10$$

Yes, the rate of change is the same when I check pairs of inputs and corresponding outputs. Each time it is equal to 10. Since the rate of change is the same, I know it is a linear function.

b. What equation describes the function?

Using the assignment of 2 to 0.2:

$$2 = 10(0.2) + b$$
$$2 = 2 + b$$
$$0 = b$$

The equation that describes the function is $y = 10x$.

c. What will the graph of the function look like? Explain.

The graph of the function will be a line. Since the function is a linear function that can be described by the equation $y = 10x$, it will graph as a line because equations of the form $y = mx + b$ graph as lines.

4. Martin says that you only need to check the first and last input and output values to determine if the function is linear. Is he correct? Explain. Hint: Show an example with a table that is not a function.

No, he is not correct. For example, determine if the following input and outputs in the table is a function.

Input	Output
1	9
2	10
3	12

Using the first and last input and output the rate of change is

$$\frac{9-12}{1-3} = \frac{-3}{-2}$$
$$= \frac{3}{2}$$

But when you use the first two input and outputs the rate of change is

$$\frac{9-10}{1-2} = \frac{-1}{-1}$$
$$= 1$$

Note to teacher: Accept any example where rate of change is different for any two inputs and outputs.

5. Is the following graph a graph of a linear function? How would you determine if it is a linear function?

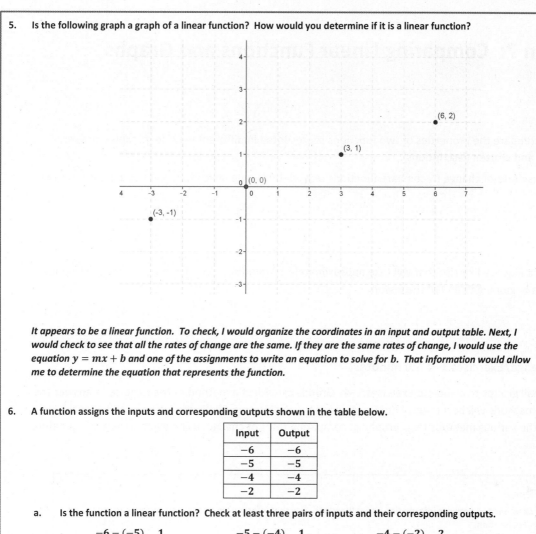

It appears to be a linear function. To check, I would organize the coordinates in an input and output table. Next, I would check to see that all the rates of change are the same. If they are the same rates of change, I would use the equation $y = mx + b$ and one of the assignments to write an equation to solve for b. That information would allow me to determine the equation that represents the function.

6. A function assigns the inputs and corresponding outputs shown in the table below.

Input	Output
−6	−6
−5	−5
−4	−4
−2	−2

a. Is the function a linear function? Check at least three pairs of inputs and their corresponding outputs.

$$\frac{-6 - (-5)}{-6 - (-5)} = \frac{1}{1} \qquad \frac{-5 - (-4)}{-5 - (-4)} = \frac{1}{1} \qquad \frac{-4 - (-2)}{-4 - (-2)} = \frac{2}{2}$$

$$= 1 \qquad\qquad\qquad = 1 \qquad\qquad\qquad = 1$$

Yes, the rate of change is the same when I check pairs of inputs and corresponding outputs. Each time it is equal to 1. Since the rate of change is the same, I know it is a linear function.

b. What equation describes the function?

Using the assignment of −5 to − 5:

$$-5 = 1(-5) + b$$
$$-5 = -5 + b$$
$$0 = b$$

The equation that describes the function is $y = x$.

c. What will the graph of the function look like? Explain.

The graph of the function will be a line. Since the function is a linear function that can be described by the equation $y = x$, it will graph as a line because equations of the form $y = mx + b$ graph as lines.

![lightbulb icon] **Lesson 7: Comparing Linear Functions and Graphs**

Student Outcomes

- Students compare the properties of two functions represented in different ways (e.g., tables, graphs, equations and written descriptions).
- Students use rate of change to compare functions (e.g., determining which function has a greater rate of change).

Lesson Notes

This lesson contains a Fluency Exercise that will take approximately 10 minutes. We recommend that the Fluency Exercise occur at the beginning or end of the lesson.

Classwork

Exploratory Challenge/Exercises 1–4 (20 minutes)

MP.1 Students work in small groups to complete Exercises 1–4. Groups can select a method of their choice to answer the questions and their methods will be a topic of discussion once the Exploratory Challenge is completed. Encourage students to discuss the various methods (e.g., graphing, comparing rates of change, using algebra) as a group before they begin solving.

Exercises 1–4

Each of the Exercises 1–4 provides information about functions. Use that information to help you compare the functions and answer the question.

1. Alan and Margot drive at a constant speed. They both drive the same route from City A to City B, a distance of 147 miles. Alan begins driving at 1:40 p.m. and arrives at City B at 4:15 p.m. Margot's trip from City A to City B can be described with the equation $y = 64x$, where y is the distance traveled and x is the time in hours spent traveling. Who gets from City A to City B faster?

    Student solutions will vary. Sample solution is provided.

    It takes Alan 155 minutes to travel the 147 miles. Therefore, his rate is $\frac{147}{155}$.

    Margot drives 64 miles per hour (60 minutes). Therefore, her rate is $\frac{64}{60}$.

    To determine who gets from City A to City B faster, we just need to compare their rates, in miles per minutes:

    $$\frac{147}{155} < \frac{64}{60}$$

    Since Margot's rate is faster, then she will get to City B faster than Alan.

> **Scaffolding:**
> Providing example language for students to reference will be useful. This might consist of sentence starters, sentence frames, or a word wall.

---

2. You have recently begun researching phone billing plans. Phone Company *A* charges a flat rate of $75 a month. A flat rate means that your bill will be $75 each month with no additional costs. The billing plan for Phone Company *B* is a function of the number of texts that you send that month. That is, the total cost of the bill changes each month depending on how many texts you send. The table below represents the inputs and the corresponding outputs that the function assigns.

Input (number of texts)	Output (cost of bill)
50	$50
150	$60
200	$65
500	$95

At what number of texts would the bill from each phone plan be the same? At what number of texts is Phone Company *A* the better choice? At what number of texts is Phone Company *B* the better choice?

Student solutions will vary. Sample solution is provided.

The equation that represents the function for Phone Company A is $y = 75$.

To determine the equation that represents the function for Phone Company B we need the rate of change:

$$\frac{60-50}{150-50} = \frac{10}{100}$$
$$= 0.1$$

$$\frac{65-60}{200-150} = \frac{5}{50}$$
$$= 0.1$$

$$\frac{95-65}{500-200} = \frac{30}{300}$$
$$= 0.1$$

The equation for Phone Company B is as follows:

Using the assignment of 50 to 50

$$50 = 0.1(50) + b$$
$$50 = 5 + b$$
$$45 = b$$

The equation that represents the function for Company B is $y = 0.1x + 45$.

We can determine at what point the phone companies charge the same amount by solving the system:

$$\begin{cases} y = 75 \\ y = 0.1x + 45 \end{cases}$$

$$75 = 0.1x + 45$$
$$35 = 0.1x$$
$$350 = x$$

After 350 texts are sent, both companies would charge the same amount, $75. More than 350 texts means that the bill from Company B will be larger than Company A. Less than 350 texts means the bill from Phone Company A will be larger.

3. A function describes the volume of water in gallons, y, that flows from faucet A for x minutes. The graph below is the graph of this function. Faucet B's water flow can be described by the equation $y = \frac{5}{6}x$, where y is the volume of water in gallons that flows from the faucet in x minutes. Assume the flow of water from each faucet is constant. Which faucet has a faster flow of water? Each faucet is being used to fill tubs with a volume of 50 gallons. How long will it take each faucet to fill the tub? How do you know? The tub that is filled by faucet A already has 15 gallons in it. If both faucets are turned on at the same time, which faucet will fill its tub faster?

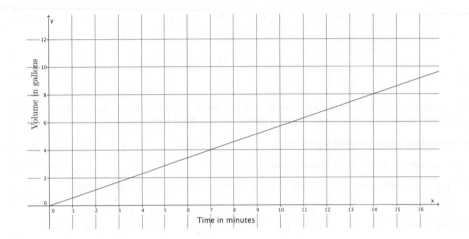

Student solutions will vary. Sample solution is provided.

The slope of the graph of the line is $\frac{4}{7}$ because $(7, 4)$ is a point on the line which represents 4 gallons of water that flows in 7 minutes. Therefore, the rate of water flow for Faucet A is $\frac{4}{7}$. To determine which faucet has a faster flow of water we can compare their rates.

$$\frac{4}{7} < \frac{5}{6}$$

Therefore, faucet B has a faster rate of water flow.

For faucet A,	For faucet B,	If the tub filled by faucet A already has 15 gallons in it,
$50 = \frac{4}{7}x$ $50\left(\frac{7}{4}\right) = x$ $\frac{350}{4} = x$ $87.5 = x$ *it will take 87.5 minutes to fill a tub of 50 gallons.*	$y = \frac{5}{6}x$ $50 = \frac{5}{6}x$ $50\left(\frac{6}{5}\right) = x$ $60 = x$ *it will take 60 minutes to fill a tub of 50 gallons.*	$50 = \frac{4}{7}x + 15$ $35 = \frac{4}{7}x$ $35\left(\frac{7}{4}\right) = x$ $61.25 = x$ *Faucet B will fill the tub first because it will take faucet A 61.25 minutes to fill the tub, even though it already has 15 gallons in it.*

4. Two people, Adam and Bianca, are competing to see who can save the most money in one month. Use the table and the graph below to determine who will save more money at the end of the month. State how much money each person had at the start of the competition.

Adam's Savings:

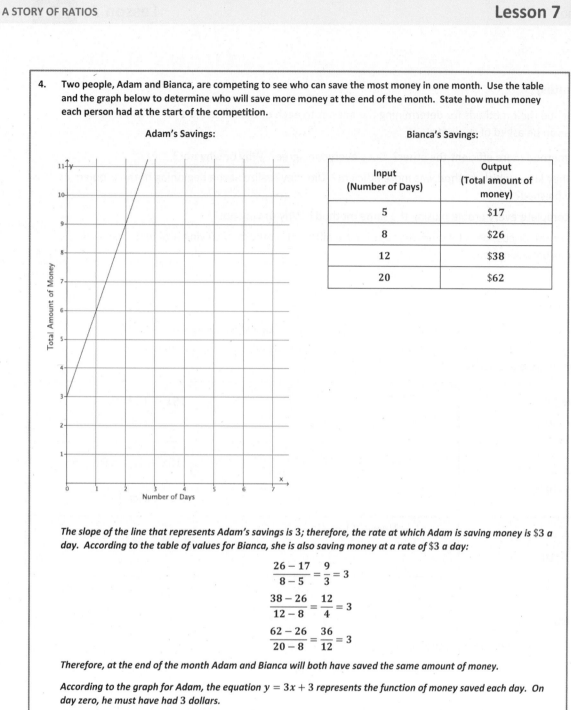

Bianca's Savings:

Input (Number of Days)	Output (Total amount of money)
5	$17
8	$26
12	$38
20	$62

The slope of the line that represents Adam's savings is 3; therefore, the rate at which Adam is saving money is $3 a day. According to the table of values for Bianca, she is also saving money at a rate of $3 a day:

$$\frac{26-17}{8-5} = \frac{9}{3} = 3$$

$$\frac{38-26}{12-8} = \frac{12}{4} = 3$$

$$\frac{62-26}{20-8} = \frac{36}{12} = 3$$

Therefore, at the end of the month Adam and Bianca will both have saved the same amount of money.

According to the graph for Adam, the equation $y = 3x + 3$ represents the function of money saved each day. On day zero, he must have had 3 dollars.

The equation that represents the function of money saved each day for Bianca is $y = 3x + 2$ because:

Using the assignment of 17 to 5

$$17 = 3(5) + b$$
$$17 = 15 + b$$
$$2 = b$$

The amount of money Bianca had on day zero is 2 dollars.

Discussion (5 minutes)

Ask students to describe their methods for determining the answer to each of the Exercises 1–4. The following questions and more can be asked of students:

- Was one method more efficient the other? Does everyone agree? Why or why not?
- How did they know which method was more efficient? Did they realize at the beginning of the problem or after they finished?
- Did they complete every problem using the same method? Why or why not?
- The point of the discussion is for students to compare different methods of solving problems and make connections between them.

MP.1

Fluency Exercise (10 minutes)

During this exercise students will solve nine multi-step equations. Each equation should be solved in about a minute. Consider having students work on white boards, showing you their solutions after each problem is assigned. The nine equations and their answers are below.

$2(x+5) = 3(x+6)$ $x = -8$	$-(4x+1) = 3(2x-1)$ $x = \dfrac{1}{5}$	$15x - 12 = 9x - 6$ $x = 1$
$3(x+5) = 4(x+6)$ $x = -9$	$3(4x+1) = -(2x-1)$ $x = -\dfrac{1}{7}$	$\dfrac{1}{3}(15x-12) = 9x - 6$ $x = \dfrac{1}{2}$
$4(x+5) = 5(x+6)$ $x = -10$	$-3(4x+1) = 2x-1$ $x = -\dfrac{1}{7}$	$\dfrac{2}{3}(15x-12) = 9x - 6$ $x = 2$

Closing (5 minutes)

Summarize, or ask students to summarize, the main points from the lesson:

- We know that functions can be expressed as equations, graphs, tables, and using verbal descriptions. No matter which way the function is expressed, we can compare it with another function.
- We know that we can compare two functions using different methods. Some methods are more efficient than others.

Exit Ticket (5 minutes)

Name _____   Date _____

Lesson 7: Comparing Linear Functions and Graphs

Exit Ticket

1. Brothers, Paul and Pete, walk 2 miles to school from home at constant rates. Paul can walk to school in 24 minutes.
    Pete has slept in again and needs to run to school. Pete's speed is shown in the graph.

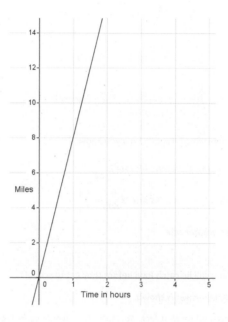

a.   Which brother walks at a greater rate? Explain how you know.

b.   If Pete leaves 5 minutes after Paul, will he catch Paul before they get to school?

Exit Ticket Sample Solutions

1. Brothers, Paul and Pete, walk 2 miles to school from home at constant rates. Paul can walk to school in 24 minutes. Pete has slept in again and needs to run to school. Pete's speed is shown in the graph.

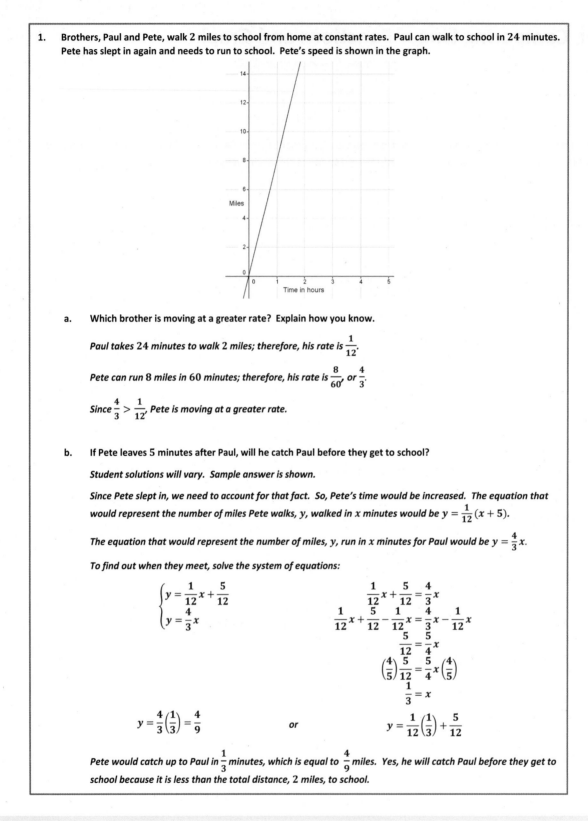

a. Which brother is moving at a greater rate? Explain how you know.

Paul takes 24 minutes to walk 2 miles; therefore, his rate is $\frac{1}{12}$.

Pete can run 8 miles in 60 minutes; therefore, his rate is $\frac{8}{60}$, or $\frac{4}{3}$.

Since $\frac{4}{3} > \frac{1}{12}$, Pete is moving at a greater rate.

b. If Pete leaves 5 minutes after Paul, will he catch Paul before they get to school?

Student solutions will vary. Sample answer is shown.

Since Pete slept in, we need to account for that fact. So, Pete's time would be increased. The equation that would represent the number of miles Pete walks, y, walked in x minutes would be $y = \frac{1}{12}(x + 5)$.

The equation that would represent the number of miles, y, run in x minutes for Paul would be $y = \frac{4}{3}x$.

To find out when they meet, solve the system of equations:

$$\begin{cases} y = \dfrac{1}{12}x + \dfrac{5}{12} \\ y = \dfrac{4}{3}x \end{cases}$$

$$\frac{1}{12}x + \frac{5}{12} = \frac{4}{3}x$$
$$\frac{1}{12}x + \frac{5}{12} - \frac{1}{12}x = \frac{4}{3}x - \frac{1}{12}x$$
$$\frac{5}{12} = \frac{5}{4}x$$
$$\left(\frac{4}{5}\right)\frac{5}{12} = \frac{5}{4}x\left(\frac{4}{5}\right)$$
$$\frac{1}{3} = x$$

$$y = \frac{4}{3}\left(\frac{1}{3}\right) = \frac{4}{9} \qquad\qquad or \qquad\qquad y = \frac{1}{12}\left(\frac{1}{3}\right) + \frac{5}{12}$$

Pete would catch up to Paul in $\frac{1}{3}$ minutes, which is equal to $\frac{4}{9}$ miles. Yes, he will catch Paul before they get to school because it is less than the total distance, 2 miles, to school.

Problem Set Sample Solutions

1. The graph below represents the distance, y, Car A travels in x minutes. The table represents the distance, y, Car B travels in x minutes. Which car is traveling at a greater speed? How do you know?

Car A:

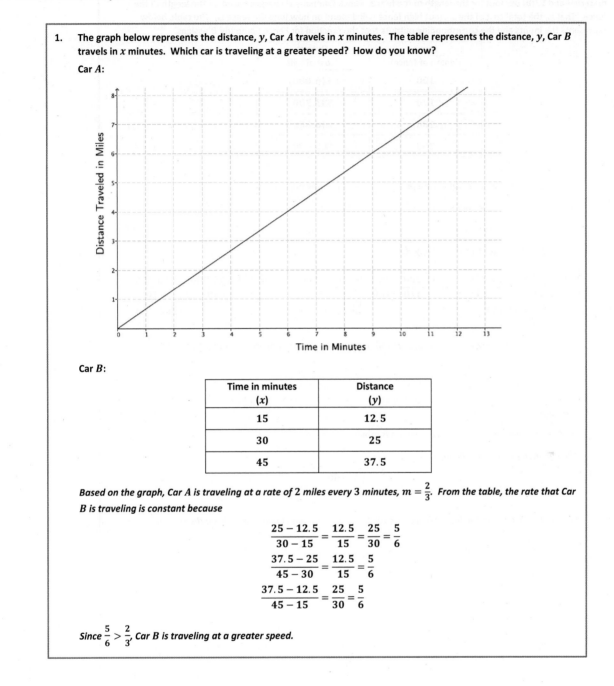

Car B:

Time in minutes (x)	Distance (y)
15	12.5
30	25
45	37.5

Based on the graph, Car A is traveling at a rate of 2 miles every 3 minutes, $m = \frac{2}{3}$. From the table, the rate that Car B is traveling is constant because

$$\frac{25 - 12.5}{30 - 15} = \frac{12.5}{15} = \frac{25}{30} = \frac{5}{6}$$

$$\frac{37.5 - 25}{45 - 30} = \frac{12.5}{15} = \frac{5}{6}$$

$$\frac{37.5 - 12.5}{45 - 15} = \frac{25}{30} = \frac{5}{6}$$

Since $\frac{5}{6} > \frac{2}{3}$, Car B is traveling at a greater speed.

2. The local park needs to replace an existing fence that is six feet high. Fence Company A charges $\$7,000$ for building materials and $\$200$ per foot for the length of the fence. Fence Company B charges based on the length of the fence. That is, the total cost of the six foot high fence will depend on how long the fence is. The table below represents the inputs and the corresponding outputs that the function for Fence Company B assigns.

Input (length of fence)	Output (cost of bill)
100	$\$26,000$
120	$\$31,200$
180	$\$46,800$
250	$\$65,000$

a. Which company charges a higher rate per foot of fencing? How do you know?

Let x represent the length of the fence and y is the total cost.

The equation that represents the function for Fence Company A is $y = 200x + 7,000$. So, the rate is 200.

The rate of change for Fence Company B:

$$\frac{26,000 - 31,200}{100 - 120} = \frac{-5,200}{-20} \qquad \frac{31,200 - 46,800}{120 - 180} = \frac{-15,600}{-60} \qquad \frac{46,800 - 65,000}{180 - 250} = \frac{-18,200}{-70}$$
$$= 260 \qquad\qquad\qquad = 260 \qquad\qquad\qquad = 260$$

Fence Company B charges a higher rate per foot because when you compare the rates, $260 > 200$.

b. At what number of the length of the fence would the cost from each fence company be the same? What will the cost be when the companies charge the same amount? If the fence you need is 190 feet in length, which company would be a better choice?

Student solutions will vary. Sample solution is provided.

The equation for Fence Company B is

$$y = 260x$$

We can find out at what point the fence companies charge the same amount by solving the system:

$$\begin{cases} y = 200x + 7000 \\ y = 260x \end{cases} \qquad\qquad \begin{aligned} 200x + 7,000 &= 260x \\ 7,000 &= 60x \\ 116.6666\ldots &= x \\ 116.6 &\approx x \end{aligned}$$

At 116.6 feet of fencing, both companies would charge the same amount (about $\$30,320$). Less than 116.6 feet of fencing means that the cost from Fence Company A will be more than Fence Company B. More than 116.6 feet of fencing means that the cost from Fence Company B will be more than Fence Company A. So, for 190 feet of fencing, Fence Company A is the better choice.

3. The rule $y = 123x$ is used to describe the function for the number of minutes needed x to produce y toys at Toys Plus. Another company, #1 Toys, has a similar function that assigned the values shown in the table below. Which company produces toys at a slower rate? Explain.

Time in minutes (x)	Toys Produced (y)
5	600
11	1,320
13	1,560

#1 Toys produces toys at a constant rate because the data in the table increases at a constant rate:

$$\frac{1,320 - 600}{11 - 5} = \frac{720}{6}$$
$$= 120$$

$$\frac{1,560 - 600}{13 - 5} = \frac{960}{8}$$
$$= 120$$

$$\frac{1,560 - 1,320}{13 - 11} = \frac{240}{2}$$
$$= 120$$

The rate of production for Toys Plus is 123 and #1 Toys is 120. Since $120 < 123$, #1 Toys produces toys at a slower rate.

4. A function describes the number of miles a train can travel, y, for the number of hours, x. The graph below is the graph of this function. Assume constant speed. The train is traveling from City A to City B (a distance of 320 miles). After 4 hours, the train slows down to a constant speed of 48 miles per hour.

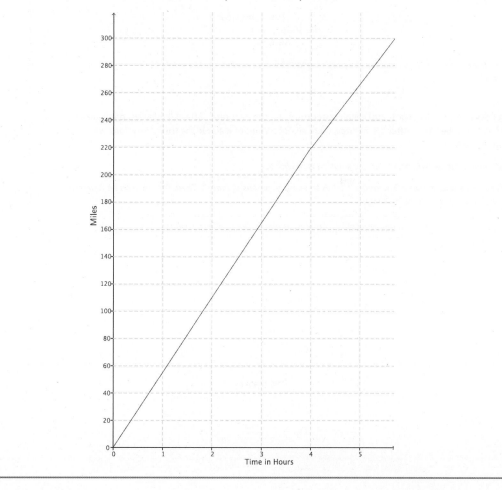

a. How long will it take the train to reach its destination?

Student solutions will vary. Sample solution is provided.

The equation for the graph is $y = 55x$. If the train travels for 4 hours at a rate of 55 miles per hour, it will have travelled 220 miles. That means it has 100 miles to get to its destination. The equation for the second part of the journey is $y = 48x$. Then,

$$100 = 48x$$
$$2.08333 \ldots = x$$
$$2 \approx x$$

This means it will take about 6 hours $(4 + 2 = 6)$ for the train to reach its destination.

b. If the train had not slowed down after 4 hours, how long would it have taken to reach its destination?

$$320 = 55x$$
$$5.8181818 \ldots = x$$
$$5.8 \approx x$$

The train would have reached its destination in about 5.8 hours had it not slowed down.

c. Suppose after 4 hours, the train increased its constant speed. How fast would the train have to travel to complete the destination in 1.5 hours?

Let m represent the new constant speed of the train, then

$$100 = m(1.5)$$
$$66.6666 \ldots = x$$
$$66.6 \approx x$$

The train would have to increase its speed to about 66.6 miles per hour to arrive at its destination 1.5 hours later.

5. a. A hose is used to fill up a 1,200 gallon water truck at a constant rate. After 10 minutes, there are 65 gallons of water in the truck. After 15 minutes, there are 82 gallons of water in the truck. How long will it take to fill up the water truck?

Student solutions will vary. Sample solution is provided.

Let x represent the time in minutes it takes to pump y gallons of water. Then, the rate can be found as follows using the following table:

Time in minutes (x)	Amount of water pumped in gallons (y)
10	65
15	82

$$\frac{65 - 82}{10 - 15} = \frac{-17}{-5}$$
$$= \frac{17}{5}$$

Since the water is pumping at constant rate, we can assume the equation is linear. Therefore, the equation for the first hose is found by:

$$\begin{cases} 10a + b = 65 \\ 15a + b = 82 \end{cases}$$

If we multiply the first equation by -1 then we have

$$\begin{cases} -10a - b = -65 \\ 15a + b = 82 \end{cases}$$

$$-10a - b + 15a + b = -65 + 82$$
$$5a = 17$$
$$a = \frac{17}{5}$$

$$10\left(\frac{17}{5}\right) + b = 65$$
$$b = 31$$

The equation for the first hose is $y = \frac{17}{5}x + 31$. If the hose needs to pump $1,200$ gallons of water into the truck, then

$$1200 = \frac{17}{5}x + 31$$
$$1169 = \frac{17}{5}x$$
$$343.8235\ldots = x$$
$$343.8 \approx x$$

It would take about 344 minutes or about 5.7 hours to fill up the truck.

b.   The driver of the truck realizes that something is wrong with the hose he is using. After 30 minutes, he shuts off the hose and tries a different hose. The second hose has a constant rate of 18 gallons per minute. How long does it take the second hose to fill up the truck?

Since the first hose has been pumping for 30 minutes, there are 133 gallons of water already in the truck. That means the new hose only has to fill up 1,067 gallons. Since the second hose fills up the truck at a constant rate of 18 gallons per minute, the equation for the second hose is $y = 18x$.

$$1,067 = 18x$$
$$59.27 = x$$

It will take the second hose 59.27 minutes (or a little less than an hour) to finish the job.

c.   Could there ever be a time when the first hose and the second hose filled up the same amount of water?

To see if the first hose and the second hose could have ever filled up the same amount of water, I would need to solve for the system:

$$\begin{cases} y = 18x \\ y = \frac{17}{5}x + 31 \end{cases}$$
$$18x = \frac{17}{5}x + 31$$
$$\frac{73}{5}x = 31$$
$$x = \frac{155}{73}$$
$$x \approx 2.12$$

The second hose could have filled up the same amount of water as the first hose at about 2 minutes.

Lesson 8: Graphs of Simple Non-Linear Functions

Student Outcomes

- Students examine the average rate of change for non-linear functions and learn that, unlike linear functions, non-linear functions do not have a constant rate of change.

- Students determine whether an equation is linear or non-linear by examining the rate of change.

Lesson Notes

In Exercises 4–10 students are given the option to graph an equation to verify their claim about the equation describing a linear or non-linear function. For this reason, students may need graph paper to complete these exercises. Students will need graph paper to complete the problem set.

Classwork

Exploratory Challenge/Exercises 1–3 (19 minutes)

Students work independently or in pairs to complete Exercises 1–3.

Exercises

1. A function has the rule so that each input of x is assigned an output of x^2.

    a. Do you think the function is linear or non-linear? Explain.

    I think the function is non-linear because non-linear expressions have variables exponents that are greater than one.

    Scaffolding:
    Students may benefit from exploring these exercises in small groups.

    b. Develop a list of inputs and outputs for this function. Organize your work using the table below. Then, answer the questions that follow.

Input (x)	Output (x^2)
-5	25
-4	16
-3	9
-2	4
-1	1
0	0
1	1
2	4
3	9
4	16
5	25

c.   Graph the inputs and outputs as points on the coordinate plane where the output is the y-coordinate.

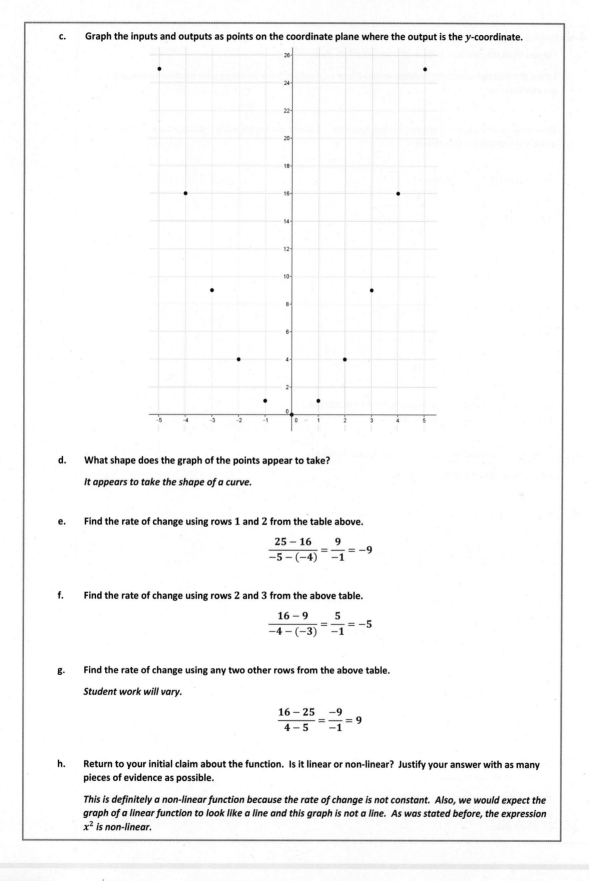

d.   What shape does the graph of the points appear to take?

It appears to take the shape of a curve.

e.   Find the rate of change using rows 1 and 2 from the table above.

$$\frac{25 - 16}{-5 - (-4)} = \frac{9}{-1} = -9$$

f.   Find the rate of change using rows 2 and 3 from the above table.

$$\frac{16 - 9}{-4 - (-3)} = \frac{5}{-1} = -5$$

g.   Find the rate of change using any two other rows from the above table.

Student work will vary.

$$\frac{16 - 25}{4 - 5} = \frac{-9}{-1} = 9$$

h.   Return to your initial claim about the function. Is it linear or non-linear? Justify your answer with as many pieces of evidence as possible.

This is definitely a non-linear function because the rate of change is not constant. Also, we would expect the graph of a linear function to look like a line and this graph is not a line. As was stated before, the expression x^2 is non-linear.

2. A function has the rule so that each input of x is assigned an output of x^3.

    a. Do you think the function is linear or non-linear? Explain.

        I think the function is non-linear because non-linear expressions have variables with exponents that are greater than one.

    b. Develop a list of inputs and outputs for this function. Organize your work using the table below. Then, answer the questions that follow.

Input (x)	Output (x^3)
-2.5	-15.625
-2	-8
-1.5	-3.375
-1	-1
-0.5	-0.125
0	0
0.5	0.125
1	1
1.5	3.375
2	8
2.5	15.625

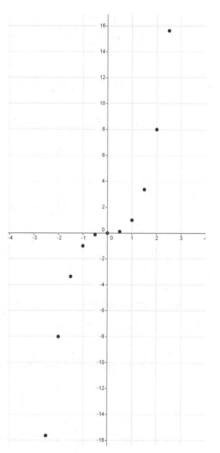

    c. Graph the inputs and outputs as points on the coordinate plane where the output is the y-coordinate.

    d. What shape does the graph of the points appear to take?

        It appears to take the shape of a curve.

    e. Find the rate of change using rows 2 and 3 from the table above.

        $$\frac{-8 - (-3.375)}{-2 - (-1.5)} = \frac{-4.625}{-0.5} = 9.25$$

    f. Find the rate of change using rows 3 and 4 from the table above.

        $$\frac{-3.375 - (-1)}{-1.5 - (-1)} = \frac{-2.375}{-0.5} = 4.75$$

    g. Find the rate of change using rows 8 and 9 from the table above.

        $$\frac{1 - 3.375}{1 - 1.5} = \frac{-2.375}{-0.5} = 4.75$$

    h. Return to your initial claim about the function. Is it linear or non-linear? Justify your answer with as many pieces of evidence as possible.

        This is definitely a non-linear function because the rate of change is not constant. Also, we would expect the graph of a linear function to look like a line and this graph is not a line. As was stated before, the expression x^3 is non-linear.

3. A function has the rule so that each input of x is assigned an output of $\frac{1}{x}$ for values of $x > 0$.

    a. Do you think the function is linear or non-linear? Explain.

        I think the function is non-linear because non-linear expressions have exponents that are less than one.

    b. Develop a list of inputs and outputs for this function. Organize your work using the table. Then, answer the questions that follow.

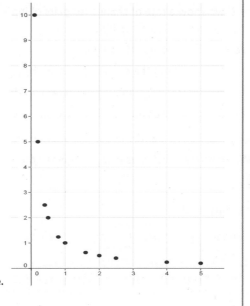

Input (x)	Output $\left(\frac{1}{x}\right)$
0.1	10
0.2	5
0.4	2.5
0.5	2
0.8	1.25
1	1
1.6	0.625
2	0.5
2.5	0.4
4	0.25
5	0.2

    c. Graph the inputs and outputs as points on the coordinate plane where the output is the y-coordinate.

    d. What shape does the graph of the points appear to take?

        It appears to take the shape of a curve.

    e. Find the rate of change using rows 1 and 2 from the table above.

$$\frac{10-5}{0.1-0.2} = \frac{5}{-0.1} = 50$$

    f. Find the rate of change using rows 2 and 3 from the table above.

$$\frac{5-2.5}{0.2-0.4} = \frac{2.5}{-0.2} = -12.5$$

    g. Find the rate of change using any two other rows from the table above.

        Student work will vary.

$$\frac{1-0.625}{1-1.6} = \frac{3.75}{-0.6} = -0.625$$

    h. Return to your initial claim about the function. Is it linear or non-linear? Justify your answer with as many pieces of evidence as possible.

        This is definitely a non-linear function because the rate of change is not constant. Also, we would expect the graph of a linear function to look like a line and this graph is not a line. As was stated before, the expression $\frac{1}{x}$ is non-linear.

Discussion (4 minutes)

- What did you notice about the rates of change in the preceding three problems?
    - *The rates of change were not all the same for each problem.*
- In Lesson 6, we learned that if the rate of change for pairs of inputs and corresponding outputs is the same for each pair, then what do we know about the function?
    - *We know the function is linear.*
- Therefore, if we know a rate of change for pairs of inputs and corresponding outputs is not the same for each pair, what do we know about the function?
    - *We know the function is non-linear.*
- What did you notice about the exponent of x in the preceding three problems?
    - *The equations $y = x^2$ and $y = x^3$ have variables with exponents that are greater than one, while the equation $y = \frac{1}{x}$ has an exponent of x that is less than one.*
- What is another way to identify equations are non-linear?
    - *We know the function is non-linear when the exponent of x is not equal to one.*

Exercises 4–10 (12 minutes)

Students work independently or in pairs to complete Exercises 4–10.

In Exercises 4–10 the rule that describes a function is given. If necessary, use a table to organize pairs of inputs and outputs, and then graph each on a coordinate plane to help answer the questions.

4. What shape do you expect the graph of the function described by $y = x$ to take? Is it a linear or non-linear function?

    I expect the shape of the graph to be a line. This function is a linear function described by the linear equation $y = x$. The graph of this function is a line.

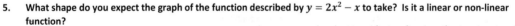

5. What shape do you expect the graph of the function described by $y = 2x^2 - x$ to take? Is it a linear or non-linear function?

    I expect the shape of the graph to be something other than a line. This function is non-linear because it does not graph as a line and the exponent of x is greater than one.

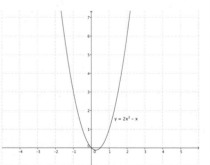

---

6. What shape do you expect the graph of the function described by $3x + 7y = 8$ to take? Is it a linear or non-linear function?

    I expect the shape of the graph to be a line. This function is a linear function described by the linear equation $3x + 7y = 8$. The graph of this function is a line.

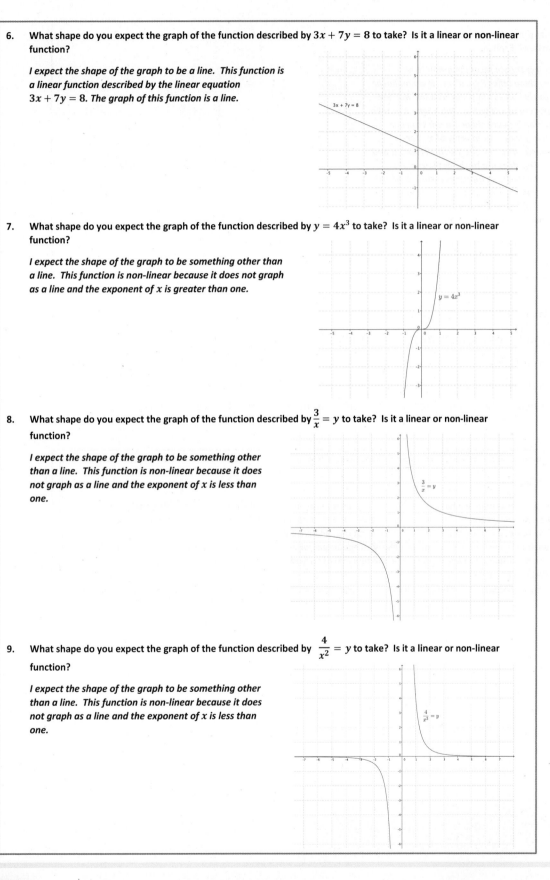

7. What shape do you expect the graph of the function described by $y = 4x^3$ to take? Is it a linear or non-linear function?

    I expect the shape of the graph to be something other than a line. This function is non-linear because it does not graph as a line and the exponent of x is greater than one.

8. What shape do you expect the graph of the function described by $\frac{3}{x} = y$ to take? Is it a linear or non-linear function?

    I expect the shape of the graph to be something other than a line. This function is non-linear because it does not graph as a line and the exponent of x is less than one.

9. What shape do you expect the graph of the function described by $\frac{4}{x^2} = y$ to take? Is it a linear or non-linear function?

    I expect the shape of the graph to be something other than a line. This function is non-linear because it does not graph as a line and the exponent of x is less than one.

10. What shape do you expect the graph of the equation $x^2 + y^2 = 36$ to take? Is it a linear or non-linear? Is it a function? Explain.

I expect the shape of the graph to be something other than a line. It is non-linear because it does not graph as a line and the exponent of x is greater than one. It is not a function because there is more than one output for any given value of x. For example, at $x = 0$ the y-value is both 6 and -6. This does not fit the definition of function because functions assign to each input exactly one output. Since there is at least one instance where an input has two outputs, it is not a function.

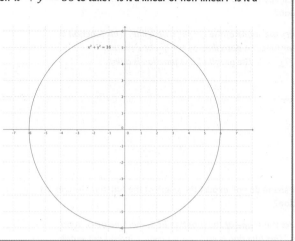

Closing (5 minutes)

Summarize, or ask students to summarize the main points from the lesson.

- Students understand that, unlike linear functions, non-linear functions do not have a constant rate of change.
- Students know that if the exponent of x is not equal to one, the graph will not be linear.
- Students expect the graph of non-linear functions to be some sort of curve.

Lesson Summary

One way to determine if a function is linear or non-linear is by inspecting the rate of change using a table of values or by examining its graph. Functions described by non-linear equations do not have a constant rate of change. Because some functions can be described by equations, an examination of the equation allows you to determine if the function is linear or non-linear. Just like with equations, when the exponent of the variable x is not equal to 1, then the equation is non-linear; therefore, the function described by a non-linear equation will graph as some kind of curve, i.e., not a line.

Exit Ticket (5 minutes)

Lesson 8:   Graphs of Simple Non-Linear Functions

Name _____   Date _____

Lesson 8: Graphs of Simple Non-Linear Functions

Exit Ticket

1. The graph below is the graph of a function. Do you think the function is linear or non-linear? Show work in your explanation that supports your answer.

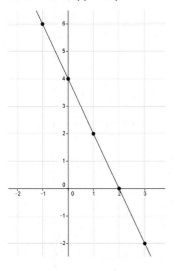

2. A function has the rule so that each input of x is assigned an output of $\frac{1}{2}x^2$. Do you think the graph of the function will be linear or non-linear? What shape do you expect the graph to take? Explain.

Exit Ticket Sample Solutions

1. The graph below is the graph of a function. Do you think the function is linear or non-linear? Show work in your explanation that supports your answer.

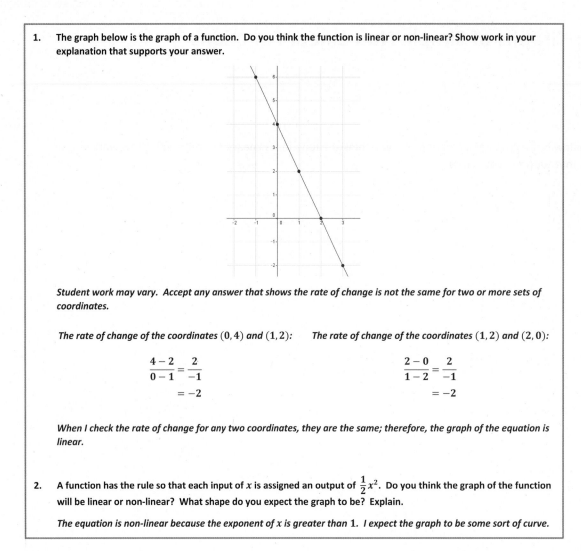

Student work may vary. Accept any answer that shows the rate of change is not the same for two or more sets of coordinates.

The rate of change of the coordinates $(0, 4)$ and $(1, 2)$:   *The rate of change of the coordinates $(1, 2)$ and $(2, 0)$:*

$$\frac{4-2}{0-1} = \frac{2}{-1}$$
$$= -2$$

$$\frac{2-0}{1-2} = \frac{2}{-1}$$
$$= -2$$

When I check the rate of change for any two coordinates, they are the same; therefore, the graph of the equation is linear.

2. A function has the rule so that each input of x is assigned an output of $\frac{1}{2}x^2$. Do you think the graph of the function will be linear or non-linear? What shape do you expect the graph to be? Explain.

The equation is non-linear because the exponent of x is greater than 1. I expect the graph to be some sort of curve.

Problem Set Sample Solutions

1. A function has the rule so that each input of x is assigned an output of $x^2 - 4$.

   a. Do you think the function is linear or non-linear? Explain.

   No, I don't think the equation is linear. The exponent of x is greater than one.

   b. What shape do you expect the graph of the function to be?

   I think the shape of the graph will be a curve.

c.   Develop a list of inputs and outputs for this function. Graph the input and outputs as points on the coordinate plane where the output is the y-coordinate.

Input (x)	Output ($x^2 - 4$)
-3	5
-2	0
-1	-3
0	-4
1	-3
2	0
3	5

d.   Was your prediction correct?

Yes, the graph appears to be taking the shape of some type of curve.

2.   A function has the rule so that each input of x is assigned an output of $\frac{1}{x+3}$.

a.   Is the function linear or non-linear? Explain.

No, I don't think the function is linear. The exponent of x is less than one.

b.   What shape do you expect the graph of the function to take?

I think the shape of the graph will be a curve.

c.   Given the inputs in the table below, use the rule of the function to determine the corresponding outputs. Graph the inputs and outputs as points on the coordinate plane where the output is the y-coordinate.

Input (x)	Output ($\frac{1}{x+3}$)
-2	1
-1	0.5
0	$0.3333\ldots..$
1	0.25
2	0.2
3	$0.16666\ldots.$

d.   Was your prediction correct?

Yes, the graph appears to be taking the shape of some type of curve.

3. Is the function that is represented by this graph linear or non-linear? Explain. Show work that supports your conclusion.

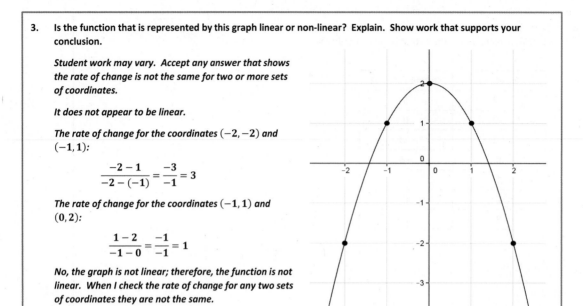

Student work may vary. Accept any answer that shows the rate of change is not the same for two or more sets of coordinates.

It does not appear to be linear.

The rate of change for the coordinates $(-2, -2)$ and $(-1, 1)$:

$$\frac{-2-1}{-2-(-1)} = \frac{-3}{-1} = 3$$

The rate of change for the coordinates $(-1, 1)$ and $(0, 2)$:

$$\frac{1-2}{-1-0} = \frac{-1}{-1} = 1$$

No, the graph is not linear; therefore, the function is not linear. When I check the rate of change for any two sets of coordinates they are not the same.

Mathematics Curriculum

Topic B:

Volume

8.G.C.9

Focus Standard:	8.G.C.9	Know the formulas for the volumes of cones, cylinders, and spheres and use them to solve real-world and mathematical problems.
Instructional Days:	3	
Lesson 9:	Examples of Functions from Geometry (E)[1]	
Lesson 10:	Volumes of Familiar Solids—Cones and Cylinders (S)	
Lesson 11:	Volume of a Sphere (P)	

In Lesson 9, students work with functions from geometry. For example, students write the rules that represent the perimeters of various regular shapes and areas of common shapes. Along those same lines, students write functions that represent the area of more complex shapes (e.g., the border of a picture frame). In Lesson 10, students learn the volume formulas for cylinders and cones. Building upon their knowledge of area of circles and the concept of congruence, students see a cylinder as a stack of circular congruent disks and consider the total area of the disks in three dimensions as the volume of a cylinder. A physical demonstration shows students that it takes exactly three cones of the same dimensions as a cylinder to equal the volume of the cylinder. The demonstration leads students to the formula for the volume of cones in general. Students apply the formulas to answer questions such as, "If a cone is filled with water to half its height, what is the ratio of the volume of water to the container itself?" Students then use what they know about the volume of the cylinder to derive the formula for the volume of a sphere. In Lesson 11, students learn that the volume of a sphere is equal to two-thirds the volume of a cylinder that fits tightly around the sphere and touches only at points. Finally, students apply what they have learned about volume to solve real-world problems where they will need to make decisions about which formulas to apply to a given situation.

---

[1] Lesson Structure Key: **P**-Problem Set Lesson, **M**-Modeling Cycle Lesson, **E**-Exploration Lesson, **S**-Socratic Lesson

Lesson 9: Examples of Functions from Geometry

Student Outcomes

- Students write rules to express functions related to geometry.
- Students review what they know about volume with respect to rectangular prisms and further develop their conceptual understanding of volume by comparing the liquid contained within a solid to the volume of a standard rectangular prism (i.e., a prism with base area equal to one).

Classwork

Exploratory Challenge 1/Exercises 1–4 (10 minutes)

Students work independently or in pairs to complete Exercises 1–4. Once students are finished, debrief that activity. Ask students to think about real-life situations that might require using the function they developed in Exercise 4. Some sample responses may include area of wood needed to make a 1-inch frame for a picture, area required to make a sidewalk border (likely larger than 1-inch) around a park or playground or the area of a planter around a tree.

Exercises

As you complete Exercises 1–4 , record the information in the table below.

	Side length (s)	Area (A)	Expression that describes area of border
Exercise 1	6	36	$64 - 36$
	8	64	
Exercise 2	9	81	$121 - 81$
	11	121	
Exercise 3	13	169	$225 - 169$
	15	225	
Exercise 4	s	s^2	$(s + 2)^2 - s^2$
	$s + 2$	$(s + 2)^2$	

1.   Use the figure below to answer parts (a)–(f).

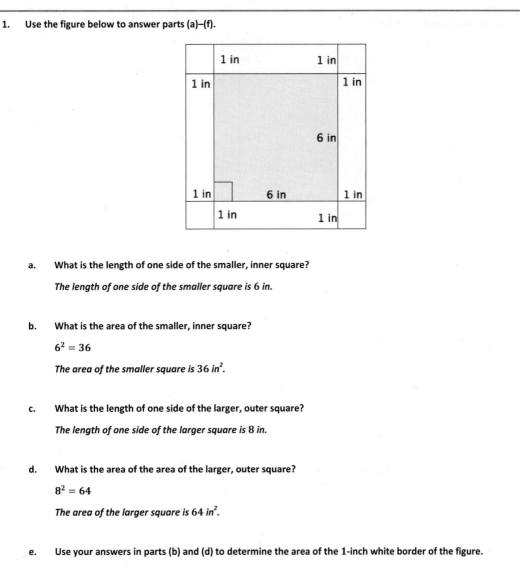

a.   What is the length of one side of the smaller, inner square?

   The length of one side of the smaller square is 6 in.

b.   What is the area of the smaller, inner square?

   $6^2 = 36$

   The area of the smaller square is 36 in².

c.   What is the length of one side of the larger, outer square?

   The length of one side of the larger square is 8 in.

d.   What is the area of the area of the larger, outer square?

   $8^2 = 64$

   The area of the larger square is 64 in².

e.   Use your answers in parts (b) and (d) to determine the area of the 1-inch white border of the figure.

   $64 - 36 = 28$

   The area of the 1-inch white border is 28 in².

f.   Explain your strategy for finding the area of the white border.

   First, I had to determine the length of one side of the larger, outer square. Since the inner square was 6 in. and the border is 1 in. on all sides, then the length of one side of the larger square is $6 + 2 = 8$ in. Then, the area of the larger square is 64 in². Then, I found the area of the smaller, inner square. Since one side length is 6 in., the area is 36 in². To find the area of the white border I needed to subtract the area of the inner square from the area of the outer square.

2. Use the figure below to answer parts (a)–(f).

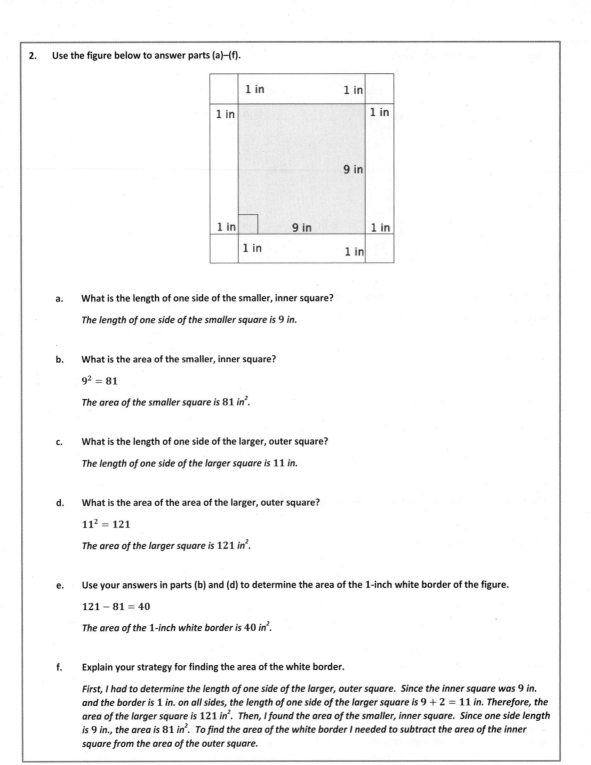

a. What is the length of one side of the smaller, inner square?

    The length of one side of the smaller square is 9 in.

b. What is the area of the smaller, inner square?

    $9^2 = 81$

    The area of the smaller square is 81 in^2.

c. What is the length of one side of the larger, outer square?

    The length of one side of the larger square is 11 in.

d. What is the area of the area of the larger, outer square?

    $11^2 = 121$

    The area of the larger square is 121 in^2.

e. Use your answers in parts (b) and (d) to determine the area of the 1-inch white border of the figure.

    $121 - 81 = 40$

    The area of the 1-inch white border is 40 in^2.

f. Explain your strategy for finding the area of the white border.

    First, I had to determine the length of one side of the larger, outer square. Since the inner square was 9 in. and the border is 1 in. on all sides, the length of one side of the larger square is $9 + 2 = 11$ in. Therefore, the area of the larger square is 121 in^2. Then, I found the area of the smaller, inner square. Since one side length is 9 in., the area is 81 in^2. To find the area of the white border I needed to subtract the area of the inner square from the area of the outer square.

3.   Use the figure below to answer parts (a)–(f).

1 in			1 in	
1 in				1 in
			13 in	
1 in		13 in		1 in
	1 in			1 in

a.   What is the length of one side of the smaller, inner square?

The length of one side of the smaller square is 13 in.

b.   What is the area of the smaller, inner square?

$13^2 = 169$

The area of the smaller square is 169 in².

c.   What is the length of one side of the larger, outer square?

The length of one side of the larger square is 15 in.

d.   What is the area of the area of the larger, outer square?

$15^2 = 225$

The area of the larger square is 225 in².

e.   Use your answers in parts (b) and (d) to determine the area of the 1-inch white border of the figure.

$225 - 169 = 56$

The area of the 1-inch white border is 56 in².

f.   Explain your strategy for finding the area of the white border.

First, I had to determine the length of one side of the larger, outer square. Since the inner square was 13 in. and the border is 1 in. on all sides, the length of one side of the larger square is $13 + 2 = 15$ in. Therefore, the area of the larger square is 225 in². Then, I found the area of the smaller, inner square. Since one side length is 13 in., the area is 169 in². To find the area of the white border I needed to subtract the area of the inner square from the area of the outer square.

4. Write a function that would allow you to calculate the area of a 1-inch white border for any sized square picture measured in inches.

a. Write an expression that represents the side length of the smaller, inner square.

Symbols used will vary. Expect students to use s or x to represent one side of the smaller, inner square. Answers that follow will use s as the symbol to represent one side of the smaller, inner square.

b. Write an expression that represents the area of the smaller, inner square.

$$s^2$$

c. Write an expression that represents the side lengths of the larger, outer square.

$$s + 2$$

d. Write an expression that represents the area of the larger, outer square.

$$(s + 2)^2$$

e. Use your expressions in parts (b) and (d) to write a function for the area A of the 1-inch white border for any sized square picture measured in inches.

$$A = (s + 2)^2 - s^2$$

Discussion (6 minutes)

This discussion is to prepare students for the volume problems with which they will work in the next two lessons. The goal is to remind students of the concept of volume using a rectangular prism, and then describe the volume in terms of a function.

- Recall the concept of volume. How do you describe the volume of a 3-dimensional figure? Give an example, if necessary.

  □ *Volume is the space that a 3-dimensional figure can occupy. The volume of a glass is the amount of liquid it can hold.*

- In Grade 6 you learned the formula to determine the volume of a rectangular prism. The volume V of a rectangular prism is a function of the edge lengths, l, w, and h. That is, the function that allows us to determine the volume of a rectangular prism can be described by the following rule:

$$V = lwh$$

- Generally, we interpret volume in the following way:

- Fill the (shell of the) solid with water and pour water into a 3-dimensional figure, in this case a standard rectangular prism, as shown.

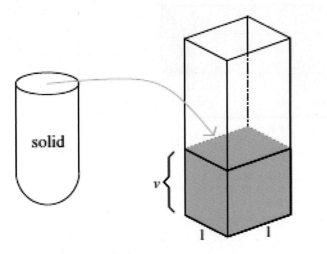

- Then the volume of the solid is the height v of the water in the standard rectangular prism. Why is the volume, v, the height of the water?

  □   *The volume is equal to the height of the water because the area of the base is 1. Thus, whatever the height, v, is multiplied by 1 will be equal to v.*

- If the height of water in the standard rectangular prism is 16.7 ft., what is the volume of the solid? Explain.

  □   *The volume of the solid would be 16.7 ft^3 because the height, 16.7, multiplied by the area of the base, 1, is 16.7.*

- There are a few basic assumptions that we make when we discuss volume. Have students paraphrase each assumption after you state it to make sure they understand the concept.

- (a) The volume of a solid is always a number ≥ 0.

- (b) The volume of a unit cube (i.e., a rectangular prism whose edges all have length 1) is by definition 1 cubic unit.

- (c) If two solids are identical, then their volumes are equal.

- (d) If two solids have (at most) their boundaries in common, then their total volume can be calculated by adding the individual volumes together. (These figures are sometimes referred to as composite solids.)

Exercises 5–6 (5 minutes)

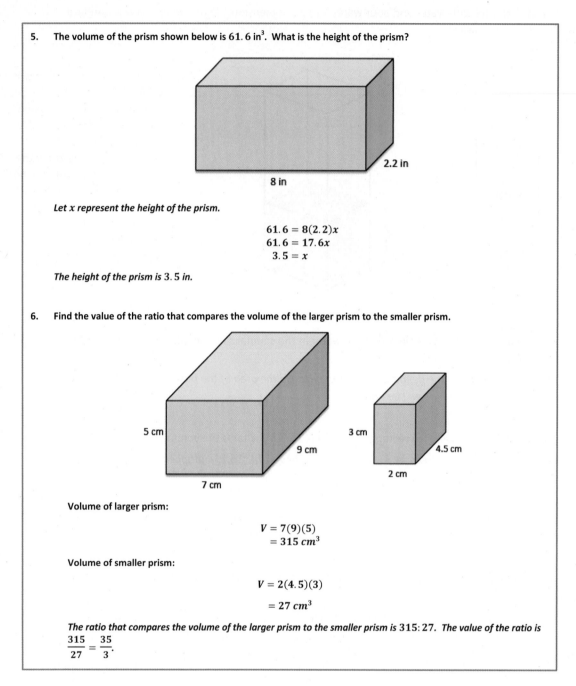

5. The volume of the prism shown below is 61.6 in^3. What is the height of the prism?

2.2 in

8 in

Let x represent the height of the prism.

$$61.6 = 8(2.2)x$$
$$61.6 = 17.6x$$
$$3.5 = x$$

The height of the prism is 3.5 in.

6. Find the value of the ratio that compares the volume of the larger prism to the smaller prism.

5 cm

9 cm

7 cm

3 cm

4.5 cm

2 cm

Volume of larger prism:

$$V = 7(9)(5)$$
$$= 315 \ cm^3$$

Volume of smaller prism:

$$V = 2(4.5)(3)$$
$$= 27 \ cm^3$$

The ratio that compares the volume of the larger prism to the smaller prism is $315\colon 27$. The value of the ratio is $\dfrac{315}{27} = \dfrac{35}{3}$.

Exploratory Challenge 2/Exercises 7–10 (14 minutes)

Students work independently or in pairs to complete Exercises 7–10.

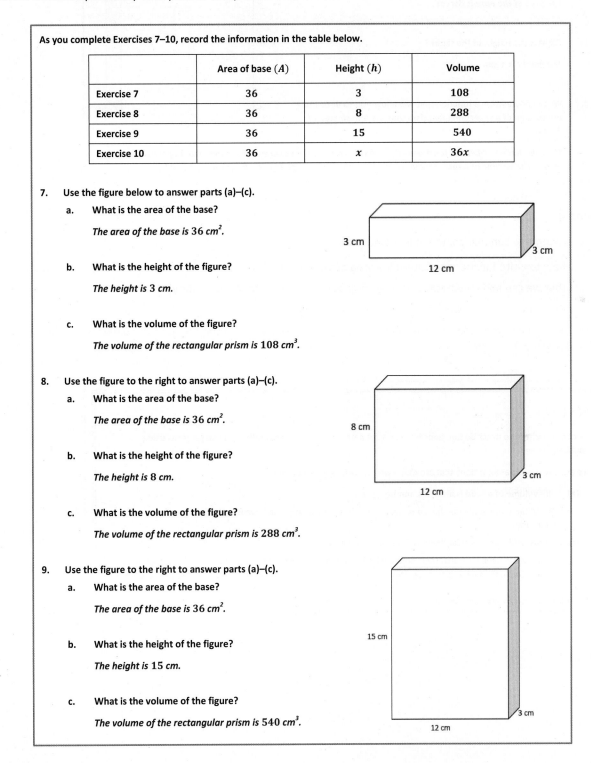

As you complete Exercises 7–10, record the information in the table below.

	Area of base (A)	Height (h)	Volume
Exercise 7	36	3	108
Exercise 8	36	8	288
Exercise 9	36	15	540
Exercise 10	36	x	$36x$

7. Use the figure below to answer parts (a)–(c).

   a. What is the area of the base?

      The area of the base is 36 cm².

   b. What is the height of the figure?

      The height is 3 cm.

   c. What is the volume of the figure?

      The volume of the rectangular prism is 108 cm³.

8. Use the figure to the right to answer parts (a)–(c).

   a. What is the area of the base?

      The area of the base is 36 cm².

   b. What is the height of the figure?

      The height is 8 cm.

   c. What is the volume of the figure?

      The volume of the rectangular prism is 288 cm³.

9. Use the figure to the right to answer parts (a)–(c).

   a. What is the area of the base?

      The area of the base is 36 cm².

   b. What is the height of the figure?

      The height is 15 cm.

   c. What is the volume of the figure?

      The volume of the rectangular prism is 540 cm³.

10. Use the figure to the right to answer parts (a)–(c).

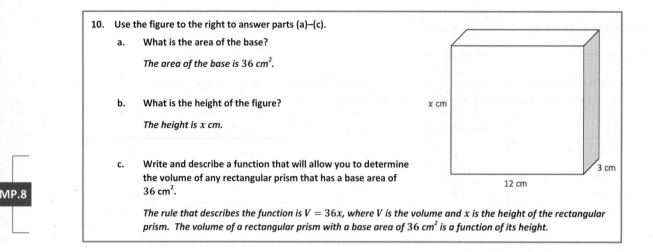

a. What is the area of the base?

The area of the base is 36 cm².

b. What is the height of the figure?

The height is x cm.

MP.8

c. Write and describe a function that will allow you to determine the volume of any rectangular prism that has a base area of 36 cm².

The rule that describes the function is $V = 36x$, where V is the volume and x is the height of the rectangular prism. The volume of a rectangular prism with a base area of 36 cm² is a function of its height.

Closing (5 minutes)

Summarize, or ask students to summarize, the main points from the lesson:

- We know how to write functions to determine area or volume of a figure.
- We know that we can add volumes together as long as they only touch at a boundary.
- We know that identical solids will be equal in volume.
- We were reminded of the volume formula for a rectangular prism, and we used the formula to determine the volume of rectangular prisms.

Lesson Summary

Rules can be written to describe functions by observing patterns and then generalizing those patterns using symbolic notation.

There are a few basic assumptions that are made when working with volume:

(a) The volume of a solid is always a number ≥ 0.

(b) The volume of a unit cube (i.e., a rectangular prism whose edges all have length 1) is by definition 1 cubic unit.

(c) If two solids are identical, then their volumes are equal.

(d) If two solids have (at most) their boundaries in common, then their total volume can be calculated by adding the individual volumes together. (These figures are sometimes referred to as composite solids.)

Exit Ticket (5 minutes)

Lesson 9:   Examples of Functions from Geometry

Name _____   Date _____

Lesson 9: Examples of Functions from Geometry

1. Write a function that would allow you to calculate the area, A, of a 2-inch white border for any sized square figure with sides of length s measured in inches.

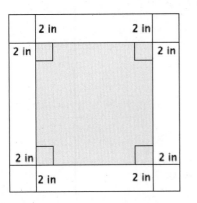

2. The volume of the rectangular prism is 295.68 in^3. What is its width?

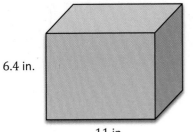

6.4 in.

11 in.

Exit Ticket Sample Solutions

1. Write a function that would allow you to calculate the area, A, of a 2-inch white border for any sized square figure with sides of length s measured in inches.

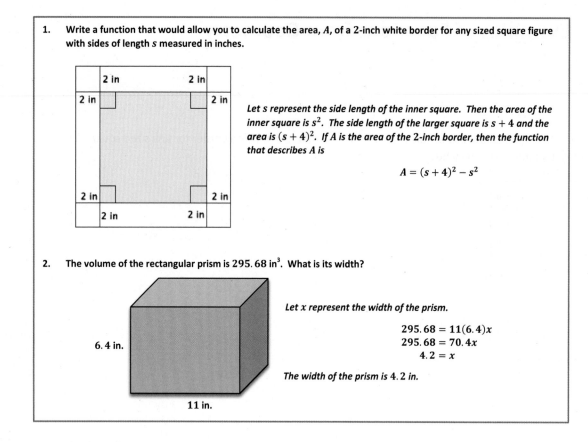

Let s represent the side length of the inner square. Then the area of the inner square is s^2. The side length of the larger square is $s + 4$ and the area is $(s + 4)^2$. If A is the area of the 2-inch border, then the function that describes A is

$$A = (s + 4)^2 - s^2$$

2. The volume of the rectangular prism is 295.68 in^3. What is its width?

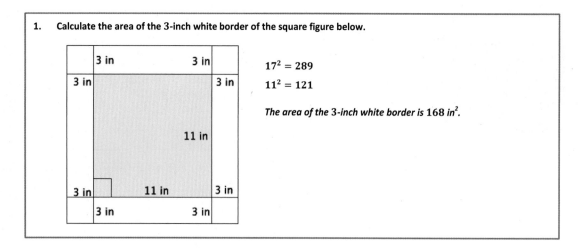

Let x represent the width of the prism.

$$295.68 = 11(6.4)x$$
$$295.68 = 70.4x$$
$$4.2 = x$$

The width of the prism is 4.2 in.

Problem Set Sample Solutions

1. Calculate the area of the 3-inch white border of the square figure below.

$$17^2 = 289$$
$$11^2 = 121$$

The area of the 3-inch white border is 168 in^2.

2. Write a function that would allow you to calculate the area A of a 3-inch white border for any sized square picture measured in inches.

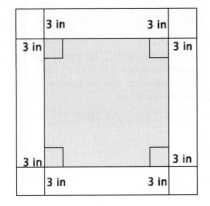

Let s represent the side length of the inner square. Then the area of the inner square is s^2. The side length of the outer square is $s + 6$, which means that the area of the outer square is $(s + 6)^2$. The function that describes the area A of the 3 inch border is

$$A = (s + 6)^2 - s^2$$

3. Dartboards typically have an outer ring of numbers that represent the number of points a player can score for getting a dart in that section. A simplified dartboard is shown below. The center of the circle is point A. Calculate the area of the outer ring. Write an exact answer that uses π (<u>do not</u> approximate your answer by using 3.14 for π).

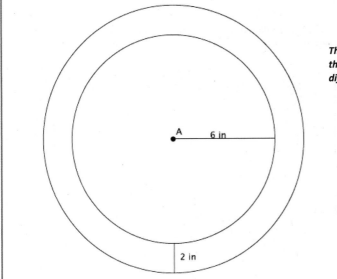

The inner ring has an area of 36π. The area of the inner ring including the border is 64π. The difference is the area of the border, 28π in^2.

4. Write a function that would allow you to calculate the area A of the outer ring for any sized dartboard with radius r. Write an exact answer that uses π (<u>do not</u> approximate your answer by using 3.14 for π).

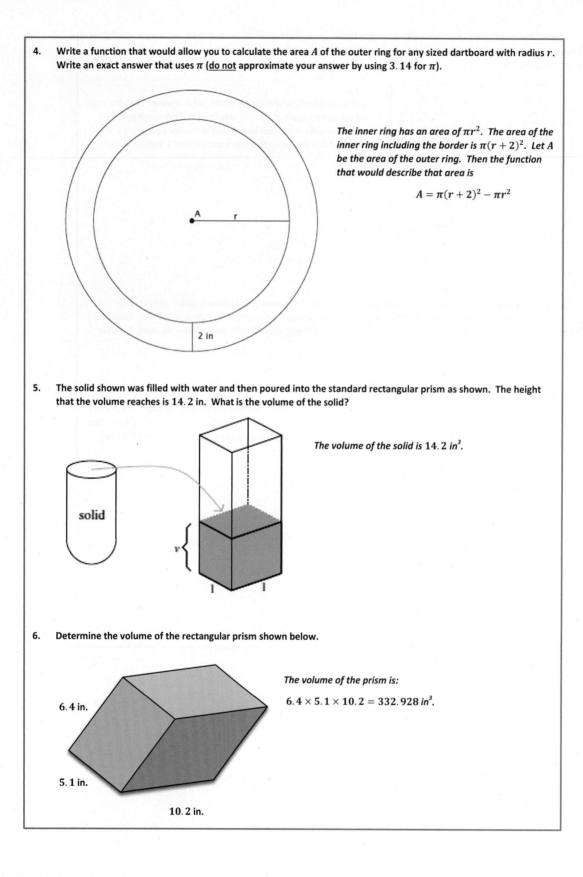

The inner ring has an area of πr^2. The area of the inner ring including the border is $\pi(r+2)^2$. Let A be the area of the outer ring. Then the function that would describe that area is

$$A = \pi(r+2)^2 - \pi r^2$$

5. The solid shown was filled with water and then poured into the standard rectangular prism as shown. The height that the volume reaches is 14.2 in. What is the volume of the solid?

The volume of the solid is 14.2 in³.

6. Determine the volume of the rectangular prism shown below.

The volume of the prism is:

$$6.4 \times 5.1 \times 10.2 = 332.928 \text{ in}^3.$$

6.4 in.

5.1 in.

10.2 in.

7. The volume of the prism shown below is 972 cm³. What is its length?

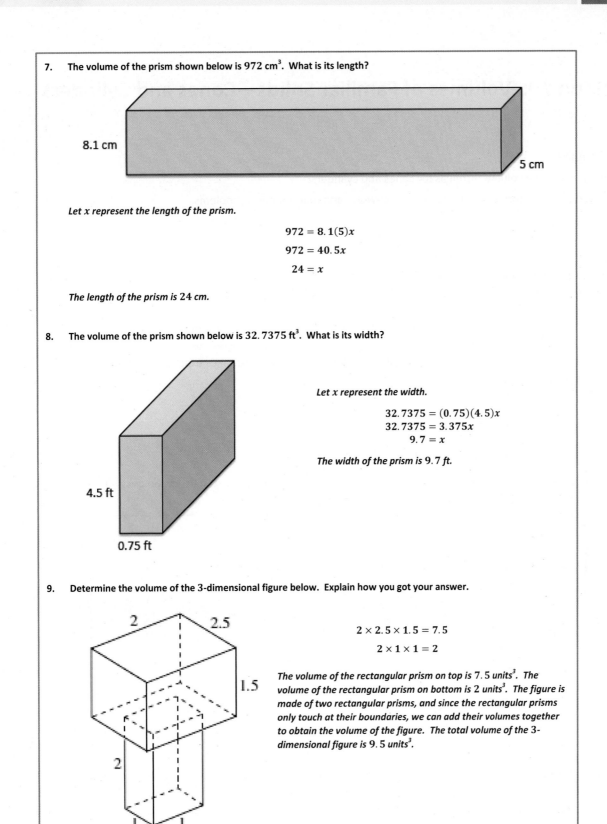

8.1 cm

5 cm

Let x represent the length of the prism.

$$972 = 8.1(5)x$$
$$972 = 40.5x$$
$$24 = x$$

The length of the prism is 24 cm.

8. The volume of the prism shown below is 32.7375 ft³. What is its width?

Let x represent the width.

$$32.7375 = (0.75)(4.5)x$$
$$32.7375 = 3.375x$$
$$9.7 = x$$

The width of the prism is 9.7 ft.

4.5 ft

0.75 ft

9. Determine the volume of the 3-dimensional figure below. Explain how you got your answer.

2   2.5

1.5

2

1   1

$$2 \times 2.5 \times 1.5 = 7.5$$
$$2 \times 1 \times 1 = 2$$

The volume of the rectangular prism on top is 7.5 units³. The volume of the rectangular prism on bottom is 2 units³. The figure is made of two rectangular prisms, and since the rectangular prisms only touch at their boundaries, we can add their volumes together to obtain the volume of the figure. The total volume of the 3-dimensional figure is 9.5 units³.

Lesson 10: Volumes of Familiar Solids—Cones and Cylinders

Student Outcomes

- Students know the volume formulas for cones and cylinders.
- Students apply the formulas for volume to real-world and mathematical problems.

Lesson Notes

For the demonstrations in this lesson you will need a stack of the same-sized note cards, a stack of the same-sized round disks, a cylinder and cone of the same dimensions, and something to fill the cone with (e.g., rice, sand, water). Demonstrate to students that the volume of a rectangular prism is like finding the sum of the areas of congruent rectangles, stacked one on top of the next. A similar demonstration will be useful for the volume of a cylinder. To demonstrate that the volume of a cone is one-third that of the volume of a cylinder with the same dimension, you will need to fill a cone with something like rice, sand, or water and show students that it takes exactly three cones to equal the volume of the cylinder.

Classwork

Opening Exercises 1–2 (3 minutes)

Students complete Exercises 1–2 independently. Revisit the Opening Exercise once the discussion below is finished.

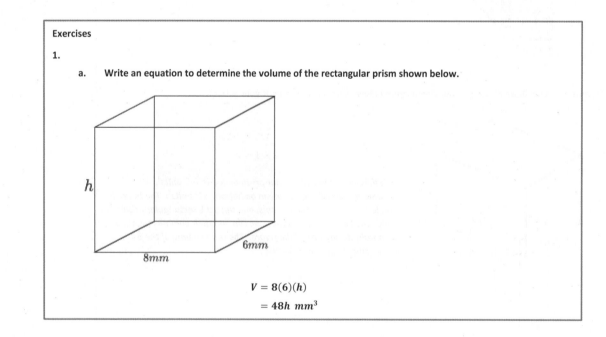

Exercises

1.

    a.   Write an equation to determine the volume of the rectangular prism shown below.

$$V = 8(6)(h)$$
$$= 48h \ mm^3$$

MP.1 & MP.7

b.   Write an equation to determine the volume of the rectangular prism shown below.

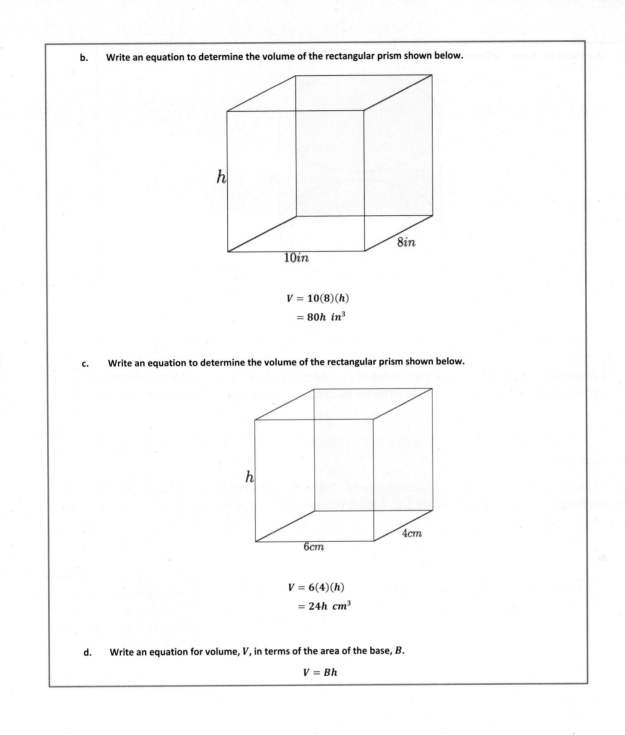

$$V = 10(8)(h)$$
$$= 80h \ in^3$$

c.   Write an equation to determine the volume of the rectangular prism shown below.

$$V = 6(4)(h)$$
$$= 24h \ cm^3$$

d.   Write an equation for volume, V, in terms of the area of the base, B.

$$V = Bh$$

MP.1
&
MP.7

2.   Using what you learned in Exercise 1, write an equation to determine the volume of the cylinder shown below.

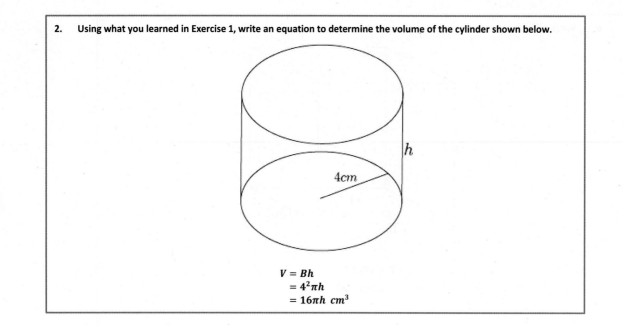

4cm

h

$V = Bh$
$\quad = 4^2\pi h$
$\quad = 16\pi h \ cm^3$

Students do not know the formula to determine the volume of a cylinder so some may not be able to respond to this exercise until after the discussion below. This is an exercise for students to make sense of problems and persevere in solving them.

Discussion (10 minutes)

- We will continue with an intuitive discussion of volume. The volume formula from the last lesson says that if the dimensions of a rectangular prism are l, w, h, then volume of the rectangular prism is $V = l \cdot w \cdot h$.

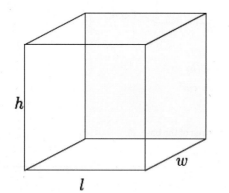

h

w

l

> Scaffolding:
> Demonstrate the volume of a rectangular prism using a stack of note cards. The volume of the rectangular prism increases as the height of the stack increases. Note that the rectangles (note cards) are congruent.

- Referring to the picture, we call the blue rectangle at the bottom of the rectangular prism the **base**, and the length of any one of the edges perpendicular to the base as the **height** of the rectangular prism. Then, the proceeding formula says:

$$V = (area \ of \ base) \cdot height$$

- Examine the volume of a cylinder with base B and height h. Is the solid (i.e., the totality of all the line segments) of length h lying above the plane, so that each segment is perpendicular to the plane, and its lower endpoint lies on the base B (as shown)?

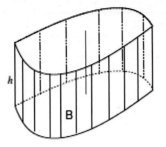

<table>
<tr><td>

Scaffolding:

Clearly stating the meanings of symbols may present challenges for new speakers of English, and as such, students may benefit from a menu of phrases to support their statements. They will require detailed instruction and support in learning the non-negotiable vocabulary terms and phrases.

</td></tr>
</table>

- Do you know a name for the shape of the base?
  - *No, it is some curvy shape.*
- Let's examine another cylinder.

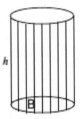

- Do we know the name of the shape of the base?
  - *It appears to be a circle.*
- What do you notice about the line segments intersecting the base?
  - *The line segments appear to be perpendicular to the base.*
- What angle does the line segment appear to make with the base?
  - *The angle appears to be a right angle.*
- When the base of a diagram is the shape of a circle and the line segments on the base are perpendicular to the base, then the shape of the diagram is called a **right circular cylinder**.

We want to use the general formula for volume of a prism to apply to this shape of a right circular cylinder.

Scaffolding:

Demonstrate the volume of a cylinder using a stack of round disks. The volume of the cylinder increases as the height of the stack increases, just like the rectangular prism. Note that the disks are congruent.

- What is the general formula for finding the volume of a prism?
  - $V = (area\ of\ base) \cdot height$
- What is the area for the base of the right circular cylinder?
  - *The area of a circle is* $A = \pi r^2$.
- What information do we need to find the area of a circle?
  - *We need to know the radius of the circle.*
- What would be the volume of a right circular cylinder?
  - $V = (\pi r^2)h$
- What information is needed to find the volume of a right circular cylinder?
  - *We would need to know the radius of the base and the height of the cylinder.*

MP.8

Lesson 10:   Volumes of Familiar Solids—Cones and Cylinders

Exercises 3–5 (8 minutes)

Students work independently or in pairs to complete Exercises 3–5.

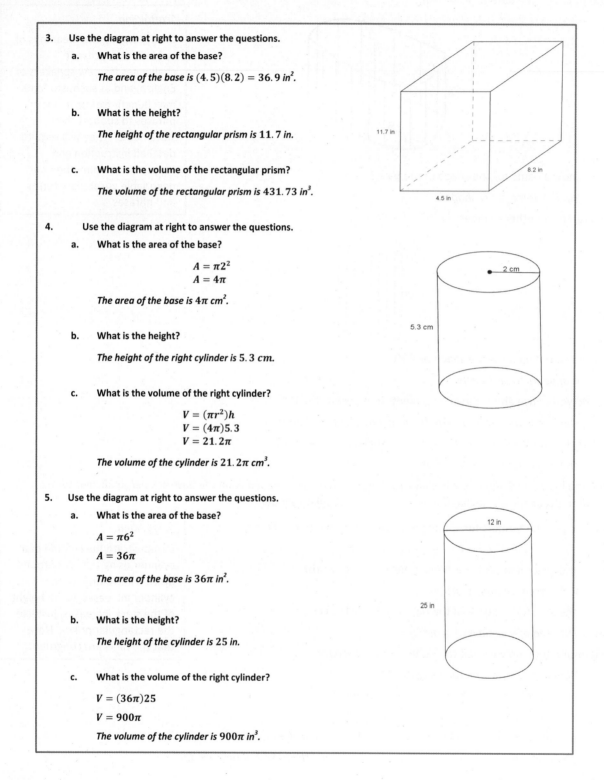

3. Use the diagram at right to answer the questions.
    a. What is the area of the base?

    The area of the base is $(4.5)(8.2) = 36.9$ in².

    b. What is the height?

    The height of the rectangular prism is 11.7 in.

    c. What is the volume of the rectangular prism?

    The volume of the rectangular prism is 431.73 in³.

4. Use the diagram at right to answer the questions.
    a. What is the area of the base?

    $$A = \pi 2^2$$
    $$A = 4\pi$$

    The area of the base is 4π cm².

    b. What is the height?

    The height of the right cylinder is 5.3 cm.

    c. What is the volume of the right cylinder?

    $$V = (\pi r^2)h$$
    $$V = (4\pi)5.3$$
    $$V = 21.2\pi$$

    The volume of the cylinder is 21.2π cm³.

5. Use the diagram at right to answer the questions.
    a. What is the area of the base?

    $$A = \pi 6^2$$
    $$A = 36\pi$$

    The area of the base is 36π in².

    b. What is the height?

    The height of the cylinder is 25 in.

    c. What is the volume of the right cylinder?

    $$V = (36\pi)25$$
    $$V = 900\pi$$

    The volume of the cylinder is 900π in³.

Discussion (10 minutes)

- Next, we introduce the concept of a cone. We start with the general concept of a cylinder. Let P be a point in the plane that contains the top of a cylinder or height, h. Then the totality of all the segments joining P to a point on the base B is a solid, called a cone with base B and height h. The point P is the top vertex of the cone. Here are two examples of such cones:

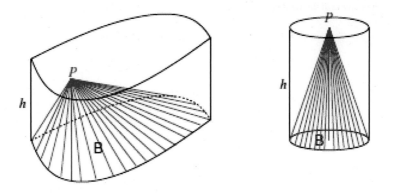

- Let's examine the diagram on the right more closely. What is the shape of the base?
    - *It appears to the shape of a circle.*
- Where does the line segment from the vertex to the base appear to intersect the base?
    - *It appears to intersect at the center of the circle.*
- What type of angle do the line segment and base appear to make?
    - *It appears to be a right angle.*
- If the vertex of a circular cone happens to lie on the line perpendicular to the circular base at its center, then the cone is called a *right circular cone*.
- We want to develop a general formula for volume of right circular cones from our general formula for cylinders.
- If we were to fill a cone of height, h, and radius, r, with rice (or sand or water), how many cones do you think it would take to fill up a cylinder of the same height, h, and radius, r?

Show students a cone filled with rice (or sand or water). Show students the cylinder of the same height and radius. Give students time to make a conjecture about how many cones it will take to fill the cylinder. Ask students to share their guesses and their reasoning to justify their claims. Consider having the class vote on the correct answer before the demonstration or showing the video. Demonstrate that it would take the volume of three cones to fill up the cylinder or show the following short, 1 minute video http://youtu.be/0ZACAU4SGyM.

- What would the general formula for the volume of a right cone be? Explain.

Provide students time to work in pairs to develop the formula for the volume of a cone.

- *Since it took 3 cones to fill up a cylinder with the same dimensions, then the volume of the cone is one-third that of the cylinder. We know the volume for a cylinder already, so the cone's volume will be $\frac{1}{3}$ of the volume of a cylinder with the same base and same height. Therefore, the formula will be*

    $V = \frac{1}{3}(\pi r^2)h.$

Exercises 6–8 (5 minutes)

Students work independently or in pairs to complete Exercises 6–8 using the general formula for the volume of a cone. Exercise 8 is a challenge problem.

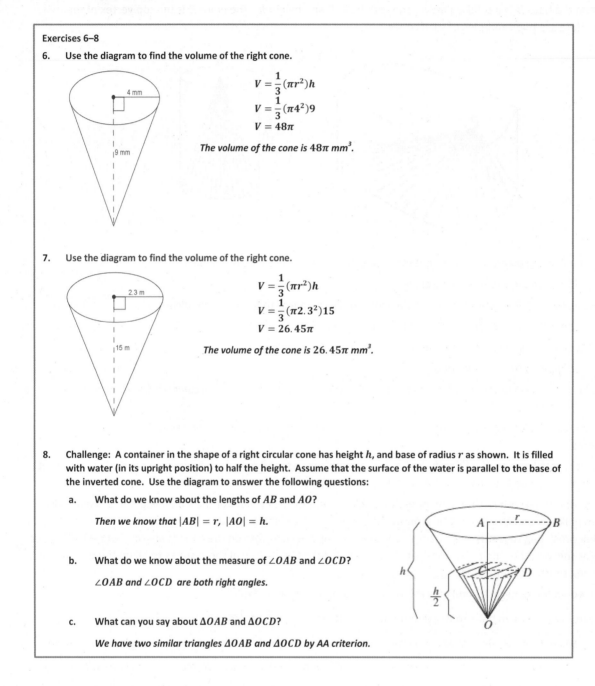

Exercises 6–8

6. Use the diagram to find the volume of the right cone.

$$V = \frac{1}{3}(\pi r^2)h$$
$$V = \frac{1}{3}(\pi 4^2)9$$
$$V = 48\pi$$

The volume of the cone is 48π mm³.

7. Use the diagram to find the volume of the right cone.

$$V = \frac{1}{3}(\pi r^2)h$$
$$V = \frac{1}{3}(\pi 2.3^2)15$$
$$V = 26.45\pi$$

The volume of the cone is 26.45π mm³.

8. Challenge: A container in the shape of a right circular cone has height h, and base of radius r as shown. It is filled with water (in its upright position) to half the height. Assume that the surface of the water is parallel to the base of the inverted cone. Use the diagram to answer the following questions:

    a. What do we know about the lengths of AB and AO?

    Then we know that $|AB| = r$, $|AO| = h$.

    b. What do we know about the measure of $\angle OAB$ and $\angle OCD$?

    $\angle OAB$ and $\angle OCD$ are both right angles.

    c. What can you say about $\triangle OAB$ and $\triangle OCD$?

    We have two similar triangles $\triangle OAB$ and $\triangle OCD$ by AA criterion.

> d. What is the ratio of the volume of water to the volume of the container itself?
>
> *Since* $\frac{|AB|}{|CD|} = \frac{|AO|}{|CO|}$, *and* $|OA| = 2|OC|$, *we have* $\frac{|AB|}{|CD|} = \frac{2|OC|}{|CO|}$.
>
> *Then* $|AB| = 2|CD|$.
>
> *Using the volume formula, we have* $V = \frac{1}{3}\pi|AB|^2|AO|$.
>
> $V = \frac{1}{3}\pi(2|CD|^2)2|OC|$
>
> $V = 8\left(\frac{1}{3}\pi|CD|^2|OC|\right)$, *where* $\frac{1}{3}\pi|CD|^2|OC|$ *gives the volume of the portion of the container that is filled with water.*
>
> *Therefore, the volume of the water to the volume of the container is* $8:1$.

Closing (4 minutes)

Summarize, or ask students to summarize, the main points from the lesson:

- Students know the volume formulas for right circular cylinders.
- Students know the volume formula for right cones with relation to right circular cylinders.
- Students can apply the formulas for volume of right circular cylinders and cones.

Lesson Summary

The formula to find the volume V, of a right circular cylinder is $V = \pi r^2 h = Bh$, where B is the area of the base.

The formula to find the volume of a cone is directly related to that of the cylinder. Given a right circular cylinder with radius r and height h, the volume of a cone with those same dimensions is exaclty one-third of the cylinder.

The formula for the volume V, of a cone is $V = \frac{1}{3}\pi r^2 h = \frac{1}{3}Bh$, where B is the area of the base.

Exit Ticket (5 minutes)

Name _____   Date _____

Lesson 10: Volumes of Familiar Solids – Cones and Cylinders

Exit Ticket

1. Use the diagram to find the total volume of the three cones shown below.

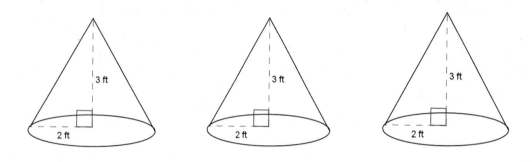

2. Use the diagram below to determine which has the greater volume, the cone or the cylinder?

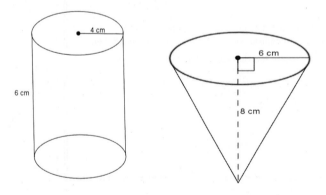

Exit Ticket Sample Solutions

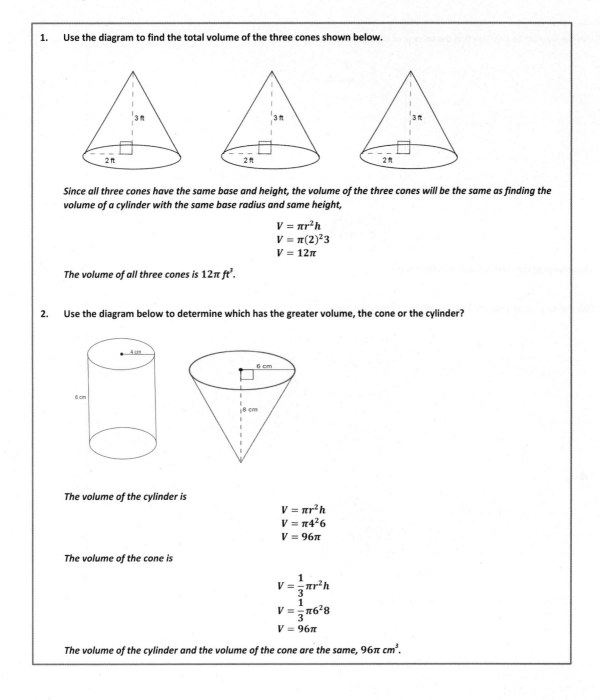

1. Use the diagram to find the total volume of the three cones shown below.

Since all three cones have the same base and height, the volume of the three cones will be the same as finding the volume of a cylinder with the same base radius and same height,

$$V = \pi r^2 h$$
$$V = \pi (2)^2 3$$
$$V = 12\pi$$

The volume of all three cones is 12π ft³.

2. Use the diagram below to determine which has the greater volume, the cone or the cylinder?

The volume of the cylinder is

$$V = \pi r^2 h$$
$$V = \pi 4^2 6$$
$$V = 96\pi$$

The volume of the cone is

$$V = \frac{1}{3}\pi r^2 h$$
$$V = \frac{1}{3}\pi 6^2 8$$
$$V = 96\pi$$

The volume of the cylinder and the volume of the cone are the same, 96π cm³.

Problem Set Sample Solutions

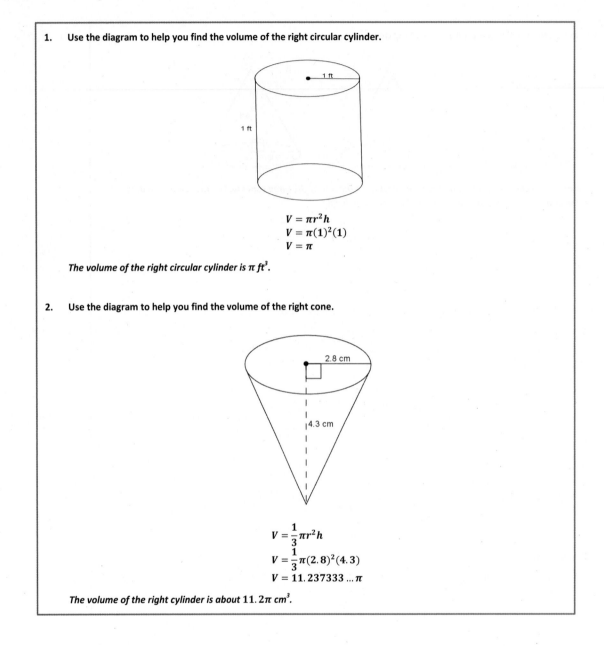

1. Use the diagram to help you find the volume of the right circular cylinder.

$$V = \pi r^2 h$$
$$V = \pi (1)^2 (1)$$
$$V = \pi$$

The volume of the right circular cylinder is π ft³.

2. Use the diagram to help you find the volume of the right cone.

$$V = \frac{1}{3} \pi r^2 h$$
$$V = \frac{1}{3} \pi (2.8)^2 (4.3)$$
$$V = 11.237333 \ldots \pi$$

The volume of the right cylinder is about 11.2π cm³.

3. Use the diagram to help you find the volume of the right circular cylinder.

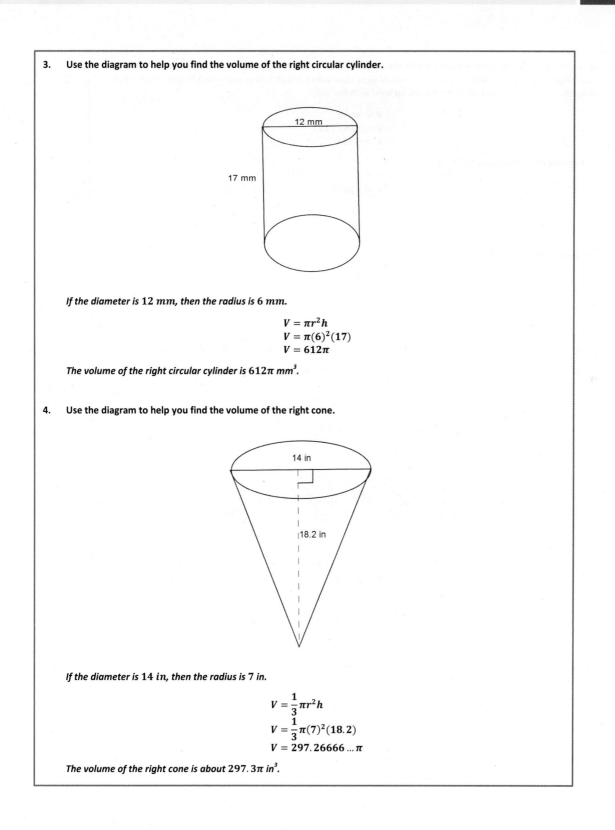

12 mm

17 mm

If the diameter is 12 mm, then the radius is 6 mm.

$$V = \pi r^2 h$$
$$V = \pi (6)^2 (17)$$
$$V = 612\pi$$

The volume of the right circular cylinder is $612\pi \text{ mm}^3$.

4. Use the diagram to help you find the volume of the right cone.

14 in

18.2 in

If the diameter is 14 in, then the radius is 7 in.

$$V = \frac{1}{3} \pi r^2 h$$
$$V = \frac{1}{3} \pi (7)^2 (18.2)$$
$$V = 297.26666 \ldots \pi$$

The volume of the right cone is about $297.3\pi \text{ in}^3$.

5. Oscar wants to fill with water a bucket that is the shape of a right circular cylinder. It has a 6-inch radius and 12-inch height. He uses a shovel that has the shape of right cone with a 3-inch radius and 4-inch height. How many shovelfuls will it take Oscar to fill the bucket up level with the top?

$$V = \pi r^2 h$$
$$V = \pi (6)^2 (12)$$
$$V = 432\pi$$

The volume of the bucket is 432π in³.

$$V = \frac{1}{3}\pi r^2 h$$
$$V = \frac{1}{3}\pi (3)^2 (4)$$
$$V = 12\pi$$

The volume of shovel is 12π in³.

$$\frac{432\pi}{12\pi} = 36$$

It would take 36 shovelfuls of water to fill up the bucket.

6. A cylindrical tank (with dimensions shown below) contains water that is 1-foot deep. If water is poured into the tank at a constant rate of $20 \ \frac{ft^3}{min}$ for 20 min., will the tank overflow? Use 3.14 to estimate π.

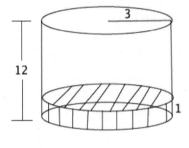

$$V = \pi r^2 h$$
$$V = \pi (3)^2 (12)$$
$$V = 108\pi$$

The volume of the tank is about 339.12 ft³.

$$V = \pi r^2 h$$
$$V = \pi (3)^2 (1)$$
$$V = 9\pi$$

There is about 28.26 ft³ of water already in the tank. There is about 310.86 ft³ of space left in the tank. If the water is poured at constant rate for 20 min., 400 ft³ will be poured into the tank and the tank will overflow.

Lesson 11: Volume of a Sphere

Student Outcomes

- Students know the volume formula for a sphere as it relates to a right circular cylinder with the same diameter and height.
- Students apply the formula for the volume of a sphere to real-world and mathematical problems.

Lesson Notes

The demonstrations in this lesson require a sphere (preferably one that can be filled with a substance like water, sand or rice), as well as a right circular cylinder with the same diameter and height as the diameter of the sphere. We want to demonstrate to students that the volume of a sphere is two-thirds the volume of the circumscribing cylinder. If this is impossible, a video link is included to show a demonstration.

Classwork

Discussion (10 minutes)

Show students the pictures of spheres below (or use real objects). Ask the class to come up with a mathematical definition on their own.

- Finally, we come to the volume of a sphere of radius r. First recall that a sphere of radius r is the set of all the points in 3-dimensional space of distance r from a fixed point, called the center of the sphere. So a sphere is by definition a surface, a 2-dimensional object. When we talk about the volume of a sphere, we mean the volume of the solid inside this surface.

Scaffolding:
Consider using a small bit of clay as the "center" and toothpicks to represent the radii of a sphere.

- The discovery of this formula was a major event in ancient mathematics. The first one to discover the formula was Archimedes (287–212 B.C.), but it was also independently discovered in China by Zu Chongshi (429–501 A.D.) and his son Zu Geng (circa 450–520 A.D.) by essentially the same method. This method has come to be known as *Cavalieri's Principle.* Cavalieri (1598–1647) was one of the forerunners of calculus, and he announced the method at a time when he had an audience.

Show students a cylinder. Convince them that the diameter of the sphere is the same as the diameter and the height of the cylinder. Give students time to make a conjecture about how much of the volume of the cylinder is taken up by the sphere. Ask students to share their guesses and their reasoning. Consider having the class vote on the correct answer before proceeding with the discussion.

- The derivation of this formula and its understanding requires advanced mathematics, so we will not derive it at this time.

If possible, do a physical demonstration where you can show that the volume of a sphere is exactly $\frac{2}{3}$ the volume of a cylinder with the same diameter and height. You could also show the following 1:17-minute video: http://www.youtube.com/watch?v=aLyQddyY8ik.

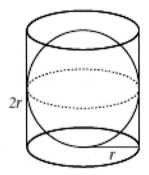

- Based on the demonstration (or video) we can say that:

$$Volume(sphere) = \frac{2}{3}\, volume(cylinder\ with\ same\ diameter\ and\ height).$$

Exercises 1–3 (5 minutes)

Students work independently or in pairs using the general formula for the volume of a sphere. Verify that students were able to compute the formula for the volume of a sphere.

Exercises 1–3

1. **What is the volume of a cylinder?**

    $V = \pi r^2 h$

2. **What is the height of the cylinder?**

    The height of the cylinder is the same as the diameter of the sphere. The diameter is $2r$.

MP.2

3. **If** $volume(sphere) = \frac{2}{3}\, volume(cylinder\ with\ same\ diameter\ and\ height)$**, what is the formula for the volume of a sphere?**

    $$Volume(sphere) = \frac{2}{3}(\pi r^2 h)$$

    $$Volume(sphere) = \frac{2}{3}(\pi r^2 2r)$$

    $$Volume(sphere) = \frac{4}{3}(\pi r^3)$$

Example 1 (4 minutes)

- When working with circular 2- and 3-dimensional figures we can express our answers in two ways. One is exact and will contain the symbol for pi, π. The other is an approximation, which usually uses 3.14 for π. Unless noted otherwise, we will have exact answers that contain the pi symbol.

- Use the formula from Exercise 3 to compute the exact volume for the sphere shown below.

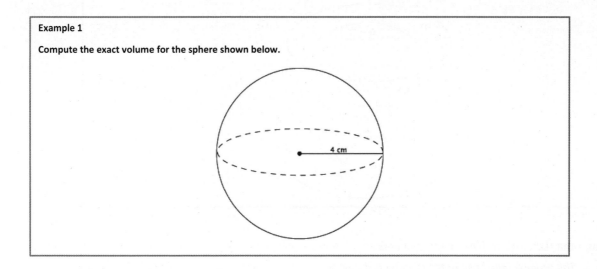

Example 1

Compute the exact volume for the sphere shown below.

4 cm

Provide students time to work, then have them share their solutions.

  □   *Sample student work:*

$$V = \frac{4}{3}\pi r^3$$
$$= \frac{4}{3}\pi(4^3)$$
$$= \frac{4}{3}\pi(64)$$
$$= \frac{256}{3}\pi$$
$$= 85\frac{1}{3}\pi$$

The volume of the sphere is $85\frac{1}{3}\pi$ cm³.

Example 2 (6 minutes)

Example 2

A cylinder has a diameter of 16 inches and a height of 14 inches. What is the volume of the largest sphere that will fit into the cylinder?

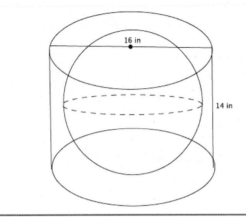

- What is the radius of the base of the cylinder?
    - *The radius of the base of the cylinder is 8 inches.*
- Could the sphere have a radius of 8 inches? Explain.
    - *No. If the sphere had a radius of 8 inches, then it would not fit into the cylinder because the height is only 14 inches. With a radius of 8 inches, the sphere would have a height of $2r$, or 16 inches. Since the cylinder is only 14 inches high, the radius of the sphere cannot be 8 inches.*
- What size radius for the sphere would fit into the cylinder? Explain.
    - *A radius of 7 inches would fit into the cylinder because $2r$ is 14, which means the sphere would touch the top and bottom of the cylinder. A radius of 7 means the radius of the sphere would not touch the sides of the cylinder, but would fit into it.*
- Now that we know the radius of the largest sphere is 7 inches. What is the volume of the sphere?
    - *Sample student work:*

$$V = \frac{4}{3}\pi r^3$$
$$= \frac{4}{3}\pi (7^3)$$
$$= \frac{4}{3}\pi (343)$$
$$= \frac{1372}{3}\pi$$
$$= 457\frac{1}{3}\pi$$

The volume of the sphere is $457\frac{1}{3}\pi$ cm³.

Lesson 11:   Volume of a Sphere

Exercises 4–8 (10 minutes)

Students work independently or in pairs to use the general formula for the volume of a sphere.

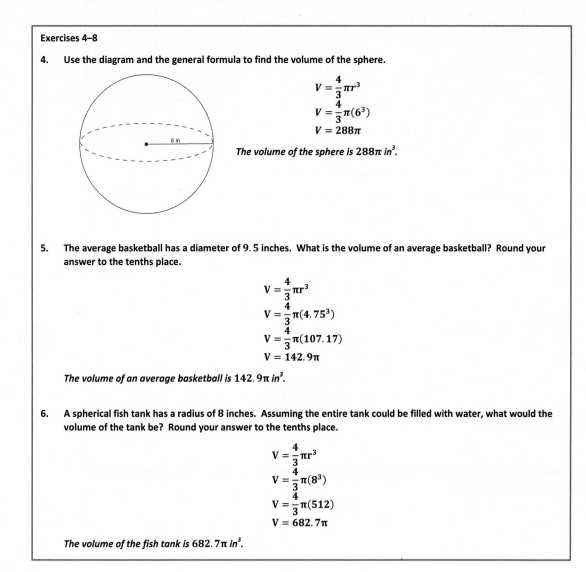

Exercises 4–8

4. Use the diagram and the general formula to find the volume of the sphere.

$$V = \frac{4}{3}\pi r^3$$
$$V = \frac{4}{3}\pi(6^3)$$
$$V = 288\pi$$

The volume of the sphere is 288π in³.

6 in

5. The average basketball has a diameter of 9.5 inches. What is the volume of an average basketball? Round your answer to the tenths place.

$$V = \frac{4}{3}\pi r^3$$
$$V = \frac{4}{3}\pi(4.75^3)$$
$$V = \frac{4}{3}\pi(107.17)$$
$$V = 142.9\pi$$

The volume of an average basketball is 142.9π in³.

6. A spherical fish tank has a radius of 8 inches. Assuming the entire tank could be filled with water, what would the volume of the tank be? Round your answer to the tenths place.

$$V = \frac{4}{3}\pi r^3$$
$$V = \frac{4}{3}\pi(8^3)$$
$$V = \frac{4}{3}\pi(512)$$
$$V = 682.7\pi$$

The volume of the fish tank is 682.7π in³.

7. Use the diagram to answer the questions.

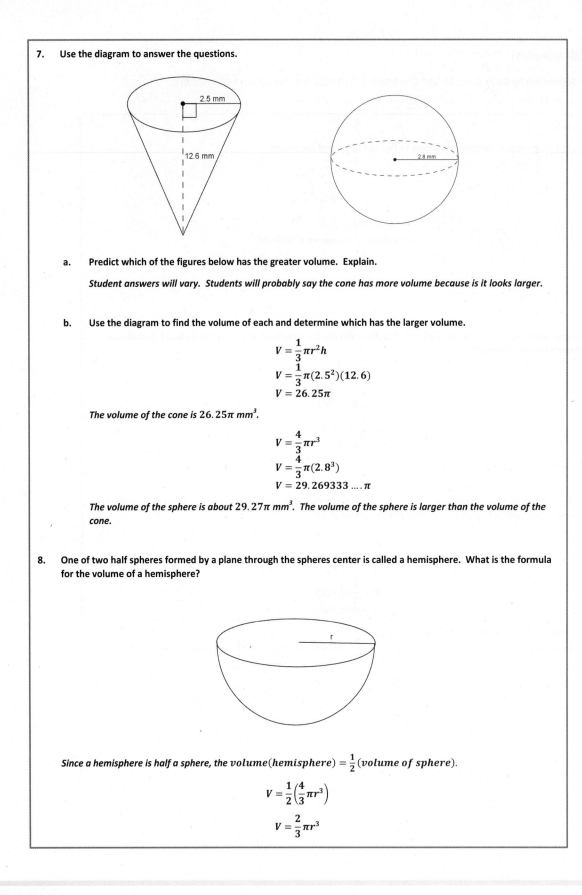

a. Predict which of the figures below has the greater volume. Explain.

    Student answers will vary. Students will probably say the cone has more volume because is it looks larger.

b. Use the diagram to find the volume of each and determine which has the larger volume.

$$V = \frac{1}{3}\pi r^2 h$$
$$V = \frac{1}{3}\pi (2.5^2)(12.6)$$
$$V = 26.25\pi$$

The volume of the cone is 26.25π mm³.

$$V = \frac{4}{3}\pi r^3$$
$$V = \frac{4}{3}\pi (2.8^3)$$
$$V = 29.269333 \ldots \pi$$

The volume of the sphere is about 29.27π mm³. The volume of the sphere is larger than the volume of the cone.

8. One of two half spheres formed by a plane through the spheres center is called a hemisphere. What is the formula for the volume of a hemisphere?

Since a hemisphere is half a sphere, the $volume(hemisphere) = \frac{1}{2}(volume\ of\ sphere)$.

$$V = \frac{1}{2}\left(\frac{4}{3}\pi r^3\right)$$
$$V = \frac{2}{3}\pi r^3$$

Closing (5 minutes)

Summarize, or ask students to summarize, the main points from the lesson:

- Students know the volume formula for a sphere with relation to a right circular cylinder.
- Students know the volume formula for a hemisphere.
- Students can apply the volume of a sphere to solve mathematical problems.

Lesson Summary

The formula to find the volume of a sphere is directly related to that of the right circular cylinder. Given a right circular cylinder with radius r and height h, which is equal to $2r$, a sphere with the same radius r has a volume that is exactly two-thirds of the cylinder.

Therefore, the volume of a sphere with radius r has a volume given by the formula $V = \frac{4}{3}\pi r^3$.

Exit Ticket (5 minutes)

Name _____   Date _____

Lesson 11: Volume of a Sphere

Exit Ticket

1. What is the volume of the sphere shown below?

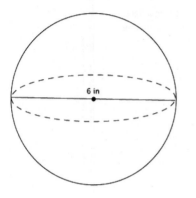

6 in

2. Which of the two figures below has the greater volume?

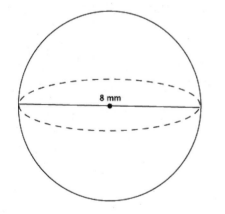

8 mm

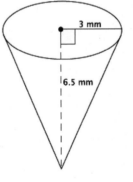

3 mm

6.5 mm

Exit Ticket Sample Solutions

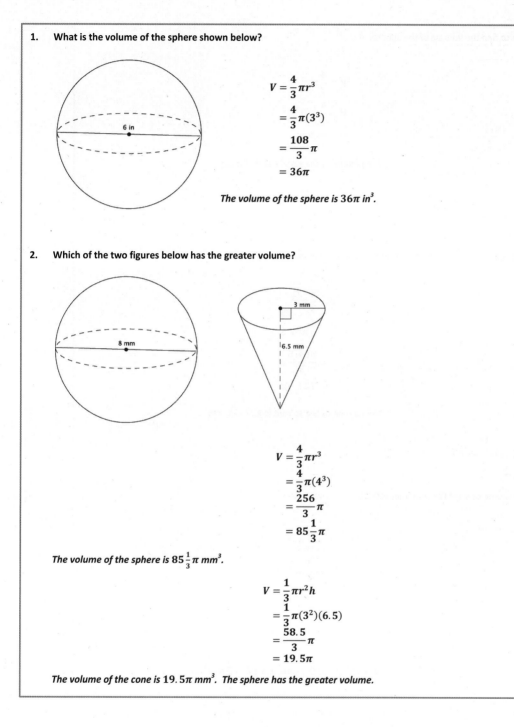

1. What is the volume of the sphere shown below?

$$V = \frac{4}{3}\pi r^3$$
$$= \frac{4}{3}\pi(3^3)$$
$$= \frac{108}{3}\pi$$
$$= 36\pi$$

The volume of the sphere is 36π in^3.

2. Which of the two figures below has the greater volume?

$$V = \frac{4}{3}\pi r^3$$
$$= \frac{4}{3}\pi(4^3)$$
$$= \frac{256}{3}\pi$$
$$= 85\frac{1}{3}\pi$$

The volume of the sphere is $85\frac{1}{3}\pi$ mm^3.

$$V = \frac{1}{3}\pi r^2 h$$
$$= \frac{1}{3}\pi(3^2)(6.5)$$
$$= \frac{58.5}{3}\pi$$
$$= 19.5\pi$$

The volume of the cone is 19.5π mm^3. The sphere has the greater volume.

Problem Set Sample Solutions

1. Use the diagram to find the volume of the sphere.

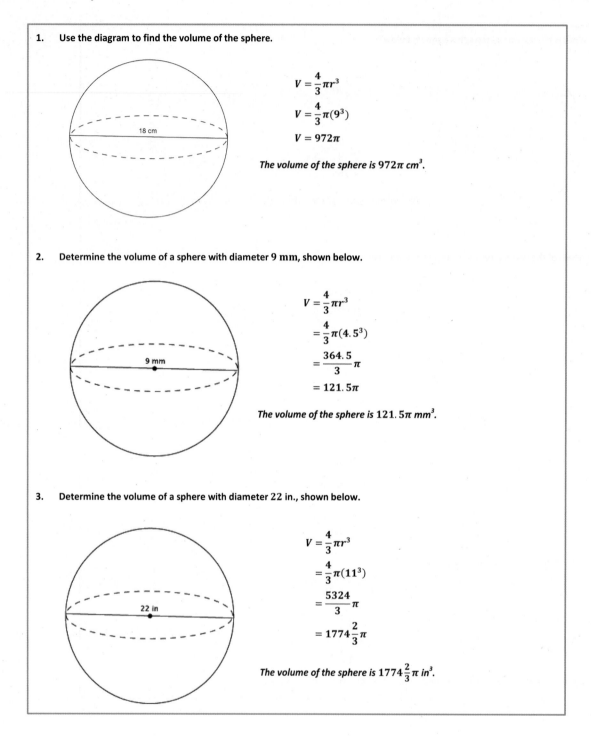

$$V = \frac{4}{3}\pi r^3$$

$$V = \frac{4}{3}\pi(9^3)$$

$$V = 972\pi$$

The volume of the sphere is 972π cm³.

2. Determine the volume of a sphere with diameter 9 mm, shown below.

$$V = \frac{4}{3}\pi r^3$$

$$= \frac{4}{3}\pi(4.5^3)$$

$$= \frac{364.5}{3}\pi$$

$$= 121.5\pi$$

The volume of the sphere is 121.5π mm³.

3. Determine the volume of a sphere with diameter 22 in., shown below.

$$V = \frac{4}{3}\pi r^3$$

$$= \frac{4}{3}\pi(11^3)$$

$$= \frac{5324}{3}\pi$$

$$= 1774\frac{2}{3}\pi$$

The volume of the sphere is $1774\frac{2}{3}\pi$ in³.

4. Which of the two figures below has the lesser volume?

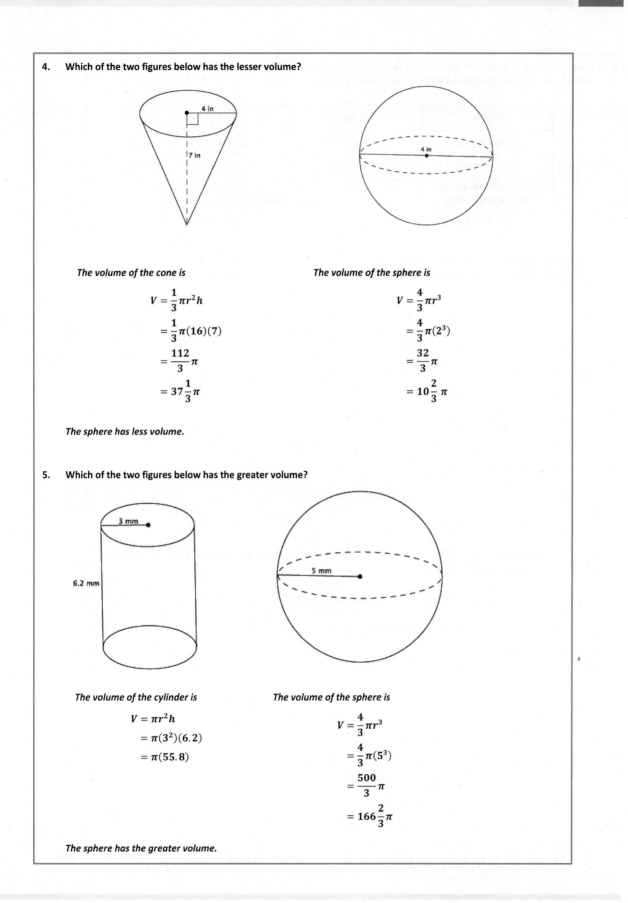

The volume of the cone is

$$V = \frac{1}{3}\pi r^2 h$$

$$= \frac{1}{3}\pi(16)(7)$$

$$= \frac{112}{3}\pi$$

$$= 37\frac{1}{3}\pi$$

The volume of the sphere is

$$V = \frac{4}{3}\pi r^3$$

$$= \frac{4}{3}\pi(2^3)$$

$$= \frac{32}{3}\pi$$

$$= 10\frac{2}{3}\pi$$

The sphere has less volume.

5. Which of the two figures below has the greater volume?

The volume of the cylinder is

$$V = \pi r^2 h$$

$$= \pi(3^2)(6.2)$$

$$= \pi(55.8)$$

The volume of the sphere is

$$V = \frac{4}{3}\pi r^3$$

$$= \frac{4}{3}\pi(5^3)$$

$$= \frac{500}{3}\pi$$

$$= 166\frac{2}{3}\pi$$

The sphere has the greater volume.

6. Bridget wants to determine which ice cream option is the best choice. The chart below gives the description and prices for her options. Use the space below each item to record your findings.

$2.00	$3.00	$4.00
1 scoop in a cup	2 scoops in a cup	3 scoops in a cup
$V \approx 4.19\ in^3$	$V \approx 8.37\ in^3$	$V \approx 12.56\ in^3$
Half a scoop on a cone filled with ice cream		A cup filled with ice cream (level to the top of the cup)
$V \approx 6.8\ in^3$		$V \approx 14.13\ in^3$

A scoop of ice cream is considered a perfect sphere and has a 2-inch diameter. A cone has a 2-inch diameter and a height of 4.5 inches. A cup is considered a right circular cylinder, has a 3-inch diameter, and a height of 2 inches.

a. Determine the volume of each choice. Use 3.14 to approximate π.

First, find the volume of one scoop of ice cream.

$$Volume\ of\ one\ scoop = \frac{4}{3}\pi(1^2)$$

The volume of one scoop of ice cream is $\frac{4}{3}\pi\ in^3$, or approximately 4.19 in^3.

The volume of two scoops of ice cream is $\frac{8}{3}\pi\ in^3$, or approximately 8.37 in^3.

The volume of three scoops of ice cream is $4\pi\ in^3$, or approximately 12.56 in^3.

$$Volume\ of\ half\ scoop = \frac{2}{3}\pi(1^3)$$

The volume of half a scoop is $\frac{2}{3}\pi\ in^3$, or approximately 2.09 in^3.

$$Volume\ of\ cone = \frac{1}{3}(\pi r^2)h$$
$$V = \frac{1}{3}(\pi 1^2)4.5$$
$$V = 1.5\pi$$

The volume of the cone is $1.5\pi\ in^3$, or approximately 4.71 in^3. Then the cone with half a scoop of ice cream on top is approximately 6.8 in^3.

$$V = \pi r^2 h$$
$$V = \pi 1.5^2(2)$$
$$V = 4.5\pi$$

The volume of the cup is $4.5\pi\ in^3$, or approximately 14.13 in^3.

b. Determine which choice is the best value for her money. Explain your reasoning.

Student answers may vary.

Checking the cost for every in^3 of each choice:

$$\frac{2}{4.19} \approx 0.47723\ldots$$
$$\frac{2}{6.8} \approx 0.29411\ldots$$
$$\frac{3}{8.37} \approx 0.35842\ldots$$
$$\frac{4}{12.56} \approx 0.31847\ldots$$
$$\frac{4}{14.13} \approx 0.28308\ldots$$

The best value for her money is the cup filled with ice cream since it costs about 28 cents for every in^3.

Lesson 11:   Volume of a Sphere

Name _____   Date _____

1.

    a.   We define x as a year between 2008 and 2013, and y as the total number of smartphones sold that year, in millions. The table shows values of x, and corresponding y values.

Year (x)	2008	2009	2010	2011	2012	2013
Number of smartphones in millions (y)	3.7	17.3	42.4	90	125	153.2

      i.   How many smartphones were sold in 2009?

     ii.   In which year were 90 million smartphones sold?

    iii.   Is y a function of x? Explain why or why not.

    b.   Randy began completing the table below to represent a particular linear function. Write an equation to represent the function he used, and complete the table for him.

Input (x)	−3	−1	0	$\frac{1}{2}$	1	2	3
Output (y)	−5		4				13

c. Create the graph of the function in part (b).

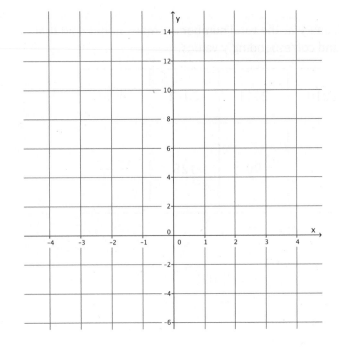

d. At NYU in 2013, the cost of the weekly meal plan options could be described as a function of the number of meals. Is the cost of the meal plan a linear or non-linear function? Explain.

8 meals: $125/week
10 meals: $135/week
12 meals: $155/week
21 meals: $220/week

2. The cost to enter and go on rides at a local water park, Wally's Water World, is shown in the graph below.

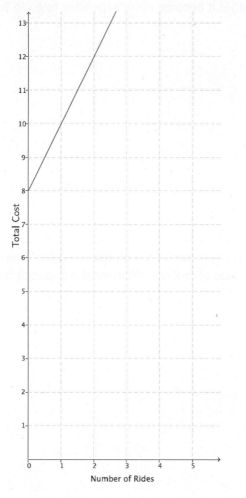

Number of Rides

A new water park just opened named Tony's Tidal Takeover. You haven't heard anything specific about how much it costs to go to this park, but some of your friends have told you what they spent. The information is organized in the table below.

# of rides	0	2	4	6
$ spent	12	13.50	15	16.50

Each park charges a different admission fee and a different fee per ride, but the cost of each ride remains the same.

a. If you only have $14 to spend, which park would you attend (assume the rides are the same quality)? Explain.

b. Another water park, Splash, opens and they charge an admission fee of $30 with no additional fee for rides. At what number of rides does it become more expensive to go to Wally's Water Park than Splash? At what number of rides does it become more expensive to go to Tony's Tidal Takeover than Splash?

c. For all three water parks, the cost is a function of the number of rides. Compare the functions for all three water parks in terms of their rate of change. Describe the impact it has on the total cost of attending each park.

3. For each part below, leave your answers in terms of π.

    a. Determine the volume for each three-dimensional figure shown below.

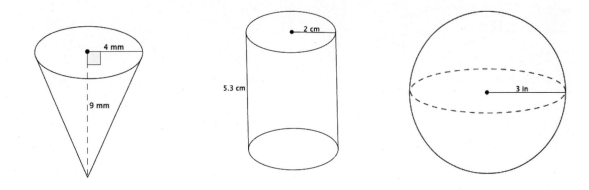

    b. You want to fill the cylinder shown below with water. All you have is a container shaped like a cone with a radius of 3 inches and a height of 5 inches; you can use this cone-shaped container to take water from a faucet and fill the cylinder. How many cones will it take to fill the cylinder?

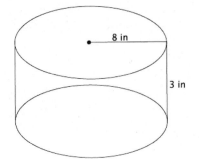

c. You have a cylinder with a diameter of 15 inches and height of 12 inches. What is the volume of the largest sphere that will fit inside of it?

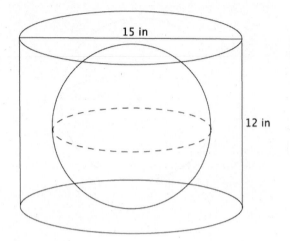

15 in

12 in

A Progression Toward Mastery

Assessment Task Item		STEP 1 Missing or incorrect answer and little evidence of reasoning or application of mathematics to solve the problem.	STEP 2 Missing or incorrect answer but evidence of some reasoning or application of mathematics to solve the problem.	STEP 3 A correct answer with some evidence of reasoning or application of mathematics to solve the problem, or an incorrect answer with substantial evidence of solid reasoning or application of mathematics to solve the problem.	STEP 4 A correct answer supported by substantial evidence of solid reasoning or application of mathematics to solve the problem.
1	a 8.F.A.1	Student makes little or no attempt to solve the problem.	Student answers at least one of the three questions correctly as 17.3 million, 2011, or yes. No explanation is provided as to why y is a function of x.	Student answers all three questions correctly as 17.3 million, 2011, and yes. Student provides an explanation as to why y is a function of x. Student may not have used vocabulary related to functions.	Student answers all three questions correctly as 17.3 million, 2011, and yes. Student provides a *compelling* explanation as to why y is a function of x and uses appropriate vocabulary related to functions (e.g., assignment, *input,* and *output*).
	b 8.F.A.1	Student makes little or no attempt to solve the problem. No function or equation is written by the student. The outputs may or may not be calculated correctly.	The equation to describe the function is not written correctly. The outputs may be correct for the function described by the student. The outputs may or may not be calculated correctly. Student may have made calculation errors. Two or more of the outputs are calculated correctly.	The equation to describe the function is written correctly. Three or more of outputs are calculated correctly. Student may have made calculation errors.	The equation to describe the function is written correctly as $y = 3x + 4$. All four of the outputs are calculated correctly as when $x = -1$, $y = 1$; when $x = \frac{1}{2}$, $y = \frac{11}{2}$; when $x = 1$, $y = 7$; and when $x = 2$, $y = 10$.

	c **8.F.A.1**	Student makes little or no attempt to solve the problem. Student may have graphed some or all of the input/outputs given.	The input/outputs do not appear to be linear. The student graphs the input/outputs incorrectly (e.g., (4,0) instead of (0,4)).	The input/outputs appear to be linear. The student may or may not have graphed the input/outputs correctly (e.g., (4,0) instead of (0,4)).	Student graphs the input/outputs correctly. The input/outputs appear to be linear.
	d **8.F.A.3**	Student does not attempt the problem or left the problem blank. Student may or may not have made a choice. No explanation is given.	Student determines the meal plan is linear or non-linear. No explanation is given or the explanation does not include any mathematical reasoning.	Student determines correctly the meal plan is non-linear. Explanation includes some mathematical reasoning. Explanation may or may include reference to the graph.	Student determines correctly that the meal plan is non-linear. Explanation includes substantial mathematical reasoning. Graph may or may not be used as part of the reasoning.
2	**a** **8.F.A.2**	Student does not attempt the problem or leaves the problem blank. Student may or may not have made a choice. No explanation is given.	Student identifies either choice. Significant calculation errors are made. Little or no explanation was given.	Student identifies either choice. Student may have made calculation errors. Explanation may or may not have included the calculation errors.	Student identifies Wally's Water World would be the better choice. Student references that for $14 they can ride three rides at Wally's but they can only ride two rides at Tony's Tidal Takeover.
	b **8.F.A.2**	Student does not attempt the problem or leaves the problem blank. No explanation is given.	Student identifies the number of rides at both parks incorrectly. Student may or may not identify functions to solve the problem. For example, student uses the table or counting method. Some attempt is made to find the function for one or both of the parks. The functions used are incorrect.	Student identifies the number of rides at one of the parks correctly. Some attempt is made to find the function for one or both of the parks. Student may or may not identify functions to solve the problem. For example, student uses the table or counting method. One function used is correct.	Student identifies that they could ride 24 rides for $30 at Wally's. Student identifies that they could ride 11 rides for $30 at Tony's. Student identifies functions to solve the problem (e.g., if x is the number of rides, $w = 2x + 8$ for the cost of Wally's and, $t = 0.75x + 12$ for the cost of Tony's).
	c **8.F.A.2**	Student does not attempt the problem or leaves the problem blank.	Student may have identified the rate of change for each park, but does so incorrectly. Student may not have compared the rate of change for each park. Student may have described the impact of the rate of change on total cost for one or two	Student correctly identifies the rate of change for each park. Student may or may not have compared the rate of change for each park. Student may have described the impact of the rate of change on total cost for all parks, but makes minor	Student correctly identifies the rate of change for each park, Wally's is 2, Tony's is 0.75, and Splash is 0. Student compares the rate of change for each park and identifies which park had the greatest rate of change (or least rate of change) as part of

Module 5:   Examples of Functions from Geometry

			of the parks, but draws incorrect conclusions.	mistakes in the description.	the comparison. Student describes the impact of the rate of change on the total cost for each park.
3	**a** 8.G.C.9	Student finds 0 to 1 of the volumes correctly. Student may or may not have included correct units. Student may have omitted π from one or more of the volumes (i.e., the volume of the cone is 48). Student does not attempt the problem or leaves it blank.	Student finds 2 out of 3 volumes correctly. Student may or may not have included correct units. Student may have omitted π from one or more of the volumes (i.e., the volume of the cone is 48).	Student finds the volumes of all three figures correctly. Student does not include the correct units. Student may have omitted π from one or more of the volumes (i.e., the volume of the cone is 48).	Student finds the volumes of all three figures correctly, that is the volume of the cone is 48π mm^3, the volume of the cylinder is 21.2π cm^3 and the volume of the sphere is 36π in^3. Student includes the correct units.
	b 8.G.C.9	Student does not attempt the problem or leaves the problem blank.	Student does not calculate the number of cones correctly. Student makes significant calculation errors. Student may have used the wrong formula for volume of the cylinder or the cone. Student may not have answered in a complete sentence.	Student may have calculated the number of cones correctly, but does not calculate the volume of the cylinder or cone correctly (e.g., volume of the cone is 192, omitting the π). Student calculates the volume of a cone correctly at 15π in^3 or the volume of the cylinder correctly at 192π in^3, but not both. Student may have used incorrect units. Student may have made minor calculation errors. Student may not answer in a complete sentence.	Student answers correctly that it will take 12.8 cones to fill the cylinder. Student calculates the volume of a cone correctly at 15π in^3 and the volume of the cylinder correctly at 192π in^3. Student answers in a complete sentence.
	c 8.G.C.9	Student does not attempt the problem or leaves the problem blank.	Student does not calculate the volume correctly. Student may have used the diameter instead of the radius for calculations. Student may have made calculation errors. Student may or may not have omitted π. Student may or may not have included the units.	Student calculates the volume correctly, but does not include the units or includes incorrect units (e.g., cm^2). Student uses the radius of 6 to calculate the volume. Student may have calculated the volume as 288 (π is omitted).	Student calculates the correct volume of 288π cm^3. Student uses the radius of 6 to calculate the volume. Student includes correct units.

Name _____   Date _____

1.

a. We define x as a year between 2008 and 2013 and y as the total number of smartphones sold that year, in millions. The table shows values of x and corresponding y values.

Year (x)	2008	2009	2010	2011	2012	2013
Number of smartphones in millions (y)	3.7	17.3	42.4	90	125	153.2

How many smartphones were sold in 2009?

17.3 MILLION SMARTPHONES WERE SOLD IN 2009

In which year were 90 million smartphones sold?

90 MILLION SMARTPHONES WERE SOLD IN 2011.

Is y a function of x? Explain why or why not.

YES IT IS A FUNCTION BECAUSE FOR EACH INPUT THERE IS EXACTLY ONE OUTPUT. SPECIFICALLY, ONLY ONE NUMBER WILL BE ASSIGNED TO REPRESENT THE NUMBER OF SMART PHONES SOLD IN THE GIVEN YEAR.

b. Randy began completing the table below to represent a particular linear function. Write an equation to represent the function he was using and compete the table for him.

Input (x)	-3	-1	0	$\frac{1}{2}$	1	2	3
Output (y)	-5	1	4	$\frac{11}{2}$	7	10	13

$y = 3x + 4$

c. Create the graph of the function in part (b).

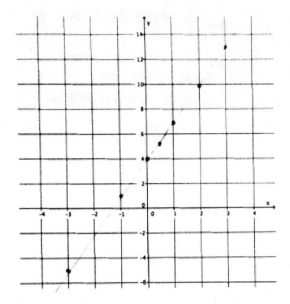

d. At NYU in 2013, the cost of the weekly meal plan options could be described as a function of the number of meals. Is the cost of the meal plan a linear or non-linear function? Explain.

8 meals: $125/week
10 meals: $135/week
12 meals: $155/week
21 meals: $220/week

$$\frac{125}{8} = 15.625 \qquad \frac{135}{10} = 13.5 \qquad \frac{155}{12} = 12.917 \qquad \frac{220}{21} = 10.476$$

THE COST OF THE MEAL PLAN IS A NON-LINEAR FUNCTION. THE COST OF EACH MEAL IS DIFFERENT BASED ON THE PLAN. FOR EXAMPLE, ONE PLAN CHARGES ABOUT $16 PER MEAL, ANOTHER PLAN CHARGES JUST $10. ALSO, WHEN THE DATA IS GRAPHED, THE POINTS DO NOT FALL IN A LINE.

2. The cost to enter and go on rides at a local water park, Wally's Water World, is shown in the graph below.

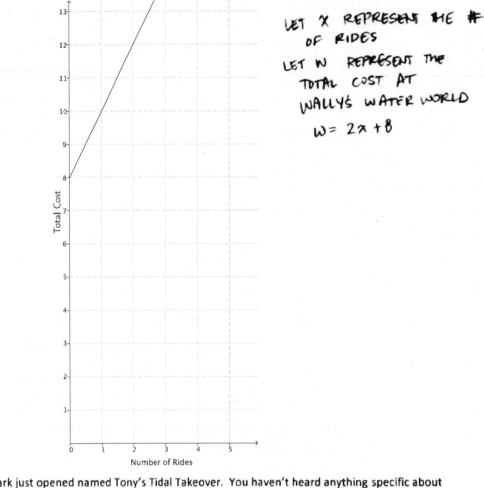

LET x REPRESENT THE # OF RIDES

LET W REPRESENT THE TOTAL COST AT WALLY'S WATER WORLD

$$W = 2x + 8$$

A new water park just opened named Tony's Tidal Takeover. You haven't heard anything specific about how much it costs to go to this park but some of your friends have told you what they spent. The information is organized in the table below; your friends told you they paid an admission fee to get in and then the same amount for each ride.

# of rides	0	2	4	6
$ spent	12	13.50	15	16.50

1.50   1.50

LET x REPRESENT THE # OF RIDES

LET T REPRESENT TOTAL COST AT TONY'S TIDAL TAKEOVER

$$T = 0.75x + 12$$

a. If you only have $14 to spend, which park would you attend (assume the rides are the same quality)? Explain.

WALLY'S
$W = 2x + 8$
$14 = 2x + 8$
$6 = 2x$
$3 = x$

TONY'S
$T = 0.75x + 12$
$14 = 0.75x + 12$
$2 = 0.75x$
$2.67 \approx x$

AT WALLY'S, YOU CAN GO ON 3 RIDES WITH $14, AT TONY'S JUST 2 RIDES. THEREFORE I WOULD GO TO WALLY'S BECAUSE YOU CAN GO ON MORE RIDES.

b.   Another water park, Splash, opens and they charge an admission fee of $30 with no additional fee
     for rides. At what number of rides does it become more expensive to go to Wally's Water Park than
     Splash? At what number of rides does it become more expensive to go to Tony's Tidal Takeover
     than Splash?

LET S REPRESENT TOTAL COST AT SPLASH,   S = 30.

WALLY'S   TONY'S.
$30 = 2x + 8$ $30 = 0.75x + 12$
$22 = 2x$ $18 = 0.75x$
$11 = x$ $24 = x$

AT WALLY'S YOU CAN GO ON 11 RIDES
WITH $30. THE 12th RIDE MAKES WALLY'S
MORE EXPENSIVE THAN SPLASH.

AT TONY'S YOU CAN GO ON 24 RIDES
WITH $30. THE 25th RIDES MAKES
TONY'S MORE EXPENSIVE THAN SPLASH.

c.   For all three water parks, the cost is a function of the number of rides. Compare the functions for all
     three water parks in terms of their rate of change. Describe the impact it has on the total cost of
     attending each park.

WALLY'S RATE OF CHANGE IS 2, $2 PER RIDE.
TONY'S RATE OF CHANGE IS 0.75, $0.75 PER RIDE.
SPLASH'S RATE OF CHANGE IS 0, $0 EXTRA PER RIDE.
WALLY'S HAS THE GREATEST RATE OF CHANGE. THAT MEANS THAT
THE TOTAL COST AT WALLY'S WILL INCREASE THE FASTEST AS WE
GO ON MORE RIDES. AT TONY'S, THE RATE OF CHANGE IS
JUST 0.75 SO THE TOTAL COST INCREASES WITH THE NUMBER
OF RIDES WE GO ON, BUT NOT AS QUICKLY AS WALLY'S.
SPLASH HAS A RATE OF CHANGE OF ZERO. THE NUMBER OF
RIDES WE GO ON DOES NOT IMPACT THE TOTAL COST AT
ALL.

3.

  a.   Determine the volume for each of the three-dimensional figures shown below.

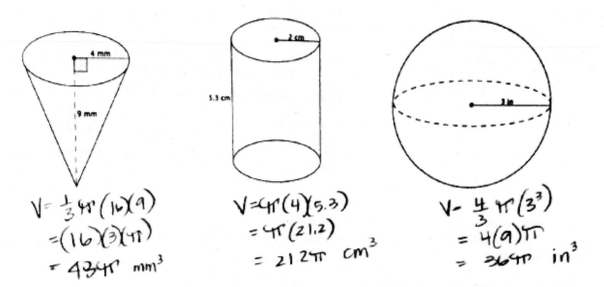

$V = \frac{1}{3}\pi (16)(9)$

$= (16)(3)(\pi)$

$= 432\pi \; mm^3$

$V = \pi(4)(5.3)$

$= \pi(21.2)$

$= 21.2\pi \; cm^3$

$V = \frac{4}{3}\pi(3^3)$

$= 4(9)\pi$

$= 36\pi \; in^3$

  b.   You want to fill the cylinder shown below with water. All you have is a container shaped like a cone with a radius of 3 inches and a height of 5 inches; you can use this cone-shaped container to take water from a faucet and fill the cylinder. How many cones will it take to fill the cylinder?

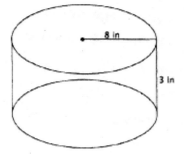

VOLUME OF CYLINDER $= \pi(64)(3)$

$= 192\pi \; in^3$

VOLUME OF CONE $= \frac{1}{3}\pi(9)(5)$

$= \frac{45}{3}\pi$

$= 15\pi \; in^3$

$\dfrac{192\pi}{15\pi} = \dfrac{192}{15} = 12.8$

IT TAKES 12.8 CONES OF THE GIVEN SIZE TO FILL THE CYLINDER.

c. You have a cylinder with a diameter of 15 cm and height of 12 cm. What is the volume of the largest sphere that will fit inside of it?

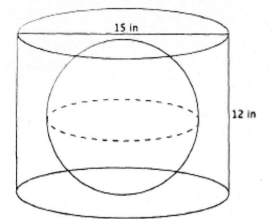

THE CYLINDER HAS RADIUS OF 7.5 cm, BUT THE HEIGHT IS JUST 12 cm. THAT MEANS THE MAXIMUM RADIUS FOR THE SPHERE IS 6 cm. ANYTHING LARGER WOULD NOT FIT IN THE CYLINDER. THEN THE VOLUME OF THE LARGEST SPHERE THAT WILL FIT IN THE CYLINDER IS

$$V = \frac{4}{3}\pi(6^3)$$
$$= \frac{4}{3}\pi(216)$$
$$= 288\pi \ cm^3.$$

Mathematics Curriculum

Student Material

Lesson 1: The Concept of a Function

Classwork

Example 1

Suppose a moving object travels 256 feet in 4 seconds. Assume that the object travels at a constant speed, that is, the motion of the object is linear with a constant rate of change. Write a linear equation in two variables to represent the situation, and use it to make predictions about the distance traveled over various intervals of time.

Number of seconds (x)	Distance traveled in feet (y)
1	
2	
3	
4	

Example 2

The object, a stone, is dropped from a height of 256 feet.   It takes exactly 4 seconds for the stone to hit the ground. How far does the stone drop in the first 3 seconds? What about the last 3 seconds? Can we assume constant speed in this situation?   That is, can this situation be expressed using a linear equation?

Number of seconds (x)	Distance traveled in feet (y)
1	
2	
3	
4	

Exercises

Use the table to answer Exercises 1–5.

Number of seconds (x)	Distance traveled in feet (y)
0.5	4
1	16
1.5	36
2	64
2.5	100
3	144
3.5	196
4	256

1. Name two predictions you can make from this table.

2. Name a prediction that would require more information.

3. What is the average speed of the object between zero and three seconds? How does this compare to the average speed calculated over the same interval in Example 1?

$$\text{Average Speed} = \frac{\text{distance traveled over a given time interval}}{\text{time interval}}$$

4. Take a closer look at the data for the falling stone by answering the questions below.

    a. How many feet did the stone drop between 0 and 1 second?

    b. How many feet did the stone drop between 1 and 2 seconds?

    c. How many feet did the stone drop between 2 and 3 seconds?

    d. How many feet did the stone drop between 3 and 4 seconds?

Lesson 1:   The Concept of a Function

e.   Compare the distances the stone dropped from one time interval to the next. What do you notice?

5.   What is the average speed of the stone in each interval 0.5 seconds? For example, the average speed over the interval from 3.5 seconds to 4 seconds is

$$\frac{\text{distance traveled over a given time interval}}{\text{time interval}} = \frac{256 - 196}{4 - 3.5} = \frac{60}{0.5} = 120 \text{ feet per second}$$

Repeat this process for every half-second interval. Then answer the question that follows.

a.   Interval between 0 and 0.5 seconds: b.   Interval between 0.5 and 1 seconds:

c.   Interval between 1 and 1.5 seconds: d.   Interval between 1.5 and 2 seconds:

e.   Interval between 2 and 2.5 seconds: f.   Interval between 2.5 and 3 seconds:

g.   Interval between 3 and 3.5 seconds:

h.   Compare the average speed between each time interval. What do you notice?

6.   Is there any pattern to the data of the falling stone? Record your thoughts below.

Time of Interval in seconds (t)	1	2	3	4
Distance Stone Fell in feet (y)	16	64	144	256

Lesson Summary

Functions are used to make predictions about real life situations. For example, a function allows you to predict the distance an object has traveled for *any* given time interval.

Constant rate cannot always be assumed. If not stated clearly, you can look at various intervals and inspect the average speed. When the average speed is the same over all time intervals, then you have constant rate. When the average speed is different, you do not have a constant rate.

$$Average\ Speed = \frac{distance\ traveled\ over\ a\ given\ time\ interval}{time\ interval}$$

Problem Set

1. A ball is thrown across the field from point A to point B. It hits the ground at point B. The path of the ball is shown in the diagram below. The x-axis shows the distance the ball travels and the y-axis shows the height of the ball. Use the diagram to complete parts (a)–(g).

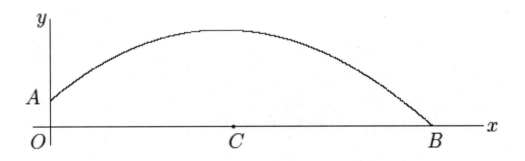

a. Suppose A is approximately 6 feet above ground and that at time $t = 0$ the ball is at point A. Suppose the length of OB is approximately 88 feet. Include this information on the diagram.

b. Suppose that after 1 second, the ball is at its highest point of 22 feet (above point C) and has traveled a distance of 44 feet. Approximate the coordinates of the ball at the following values of t: 0.25, 0.5, 0.75, 1, 1.25, 1.5, 1.75, and 2.

c. Use your answer from part (b) to write two predictions.

d. What is the meaning of the point $(88, 0)$?

e. Why do you think the ball is at point $(0, 6)$ when $t = 0$? In other words, why isn't the height of the ball zero?

f. Does the graph allow us to make predictions about the height of the ball at all points?

2. In your own words, explain the purpose of a function and why it is needed.

Lesson 2: Formal Definition of a Function

Classwork

Exercises

1. Let y be the distance traveled in time t. Use the function $y = 16t^2$ to calculate the distance the stone dropped for the given time t.

Time of Interval in seconds (t)	0.5	1	1.5	2	2.5	3	3.5	4
Distance Stone Fell in feet (y)								

   a. Are the distances you calculated equal to the table from Lesson 1?

   b. Does the function $y = 16t^2$ accurately represent the distance the stone fell after a given time t? In other words, does the function assign to t the correct distance? Explain.

2. Can the table shown below represent a function? Explain.

Input (x)	1	3	5	5	9
Output (y)	7	16	19	20	28

3. Can the table shown below represent a function? Explain.

Input (x)	0.5	7	7	12	15
Output (y)	1	15	10	23	30

4. Can the table shown below represent a function? Explain.

Input (x)	10	20	50	75	90
Output (y)	32	32	156	240	288

5. It takes Josephine 34 minutes to complete her homework assignment of 10 problems. If we assume that she works at a constant rate, we can describe the situation using a function.

   a. Predict how many problems Josephine can complete in 25 minutes.

   b. Write the two-variable linear equation that represents Josephine's constant rate of work.

c.   Use the equation you wrote in part (b) as the formula for the function to complete the table below. Round your answers to the hundredths place.

Time taken to complete problems (x)	5	10	15	20	25
Number of problems completed (y)	1.47				

After 5 minutes, Josephine was able to complete 1.47 problems, which means that she was able to complete 1 problem, then get about halfway through the next problem.

d.   Compare your prediction from part (a) to the number you found in the table above.

e.   Use the formula from part (b) to compute the number of problems completed when $x = -7$. Does your answer make sense? Explain.

f.   For this problem we assumed that Josephine worked at a constant rate. Do you think that is a reasonable assumption for this situation? Explain.

Lesson Summary

A **function** is a rule that assigns to each input exactly one output. The phrase "exactly one output" must be part of the definition so that the function can serve its purpose of being predictive.

Functions are sometimes described as an input-output machine. For example, given a function D, the input is time t and the output is the distance traveled in t seconds.

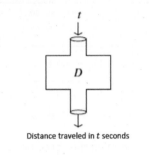

Distance traveled in t seconds

Problem Set

1. The table below represents the number of minutes Francisco spends at the gym each day for a week. Does the data shown below represent a function? Explain.

Day (x)	1	2	3	4	5	6	7
Time in minutes (y)	35	45	30	45	35	0	0

2. Can the table shown below represent a function? Explain.

Input (x)	9	8	7	8	9
Output (y)	11	15	19	24	28

3. Olivia examined the table of values shown below and stated that a possible rule to describe this function could be $y = -2x + 9$. Is she correct? Explain.

Input (x)	−4	0	4	8	12	16	20	24
Output (y)	17	9	1	−7	−15	−23	−31	−39

4. Peter said that the set of data in part (a) describes a function, but the set of data in part (b) does not. Do you agree? Explain why or why not.

a.

Input (x)	1	2	3	4	5	6	7	8
Output (y)	8	10	32	6	10	27	156	4

b.

Input (x)	−6	−15	−9	−3	−2	−3	8	9
Output (y)	0	−6	8	14	1	2	11	41

5. A function can be described by the rule $y = x^2 + 4$. Determine the corresponding output for each given input.

Input (x)	−3	−2	−1	0	1	2	3	4
Output (y)								

6. Examine the data in the table below. The inputs and outputs represent a situation where constant rate can be assumed. Determine the rule that describes the function.

Input (x)	−1	0	1	2	3	4	5	6
Output (y)	3	8	13	18	23	28	33	38

7. Examine the data in the table below. The inputs represent the number of bags of candy purchased, and the outputs represent the cost. Determine the cost of one bag of candy, assuming the price per bag is the same no matter how much candy is purchased. Then, complete the table.

Bags of Candy (x)	1	2	3	4	5	6	7	8
Cost (y)				$5	$6.25			$10

a. Write the rule that describes the function.

b. Can you determine the value of the output for an input of $x = -4$? If so, what is it?

c. Does an input of −4 make sense in this situation? Explain.

8. A local grocery store sells 2 pounds of bananas for $1. Can this situation be represented by a function? Explain.

9. Write a brief explanation to a classmate who was absent today about why the table in part (a) is a function and the table in part (b) is not.

a.

Input (x)	−1	−2	−3	−4	4	3	2	1
Output (y)	81	100	320	400	400	320	100	81

b.

Input (x)	1	6	−9	−2	1	−10	8	14
Output (y)	2	6	−47	−8	19	−2	15	31

Lesson 3: Linear Functions and Proportionality

Classwork

Example 1

In the last lesson we looked at several tables of values that represented the inputs and outputs of functions. For example:

Bags of Candy (x)	1	2	3	4	5	6	7	8
Cost (y)	$1.25	$2.50	$3.75	$5	$6.25	$7.50	$8.75	$10

Example 2

Walter walks 8 miles in two hours. What is his average speed?

Example 3

Veronica runs at a constant speed. The distance she runs is a function of the time she spends running. The function has the table of values shown below.

Time in minutes (x)	8	16	24	32
Distance ran in miles (y)	1	2	3	4

Example 4

Water flows from a faucet at a constant rate. That is, the volume of water that flows out of the faucet is the same over any given time interval. If 7 gallons of water flow from the faucet every 2 minutes, determine the rule that describes the volume function of the faucet.

Now assume that you are filling the same tub, a tub with a volume of 50 gallons, with the same faucet, a faucet where the rate of water flow is 3.5 gallons per minute. This time, however, the tub already has 8 gallons in it. Will it still take 14 minutes to fill the tub? Explain.

Time in minutes (x)	0	3	6	9	12
Total Volume in tub in gallons (y)					

Example 5

Water flows from a faucet at a constant rate. Assume that 6 gallons of water are already in a tub by the time we notice the faucet is on. This information is recorded as 0 minutes and 6 gallons of water in the table below. The other values show how many gallons of water are in the tub at the given number of minutes.

Time in minutes (x)	0	3	5	9
Total Volume in tub in gallons (y)	6	9.6	12	16.8

Exercises

1. A linear function has the table of values below. The information in the table shows the function of time in minutes with respect to mowing an area of lawn in square feet.

Number of minutes (x)	5	20	30	50
Area mowed in square feet (y)	36	144	216	360

    a. Explain why this is a linear function.

    b. Describe the function in terms of area mowed and time.

    c. What is the rate of mowing a lawn in 5 minutes?

    d. What is the rate of mowing a lawn in 20 minutes?

    e. What is the rate for mowing a lawn in 30 minutes?

    f. What is the rate for mowing a lawn in in 50 minutes?

    g. Write the rule that represents the linear function that describes the area in square feet mowed, y, in x minutes.

h. Describe the limitations of x and y.

i. What number does the function assign to 24? That is, what area of lawn can be mowed in 24 minutes?

j. How many minutes would it take to mow an area of 400 square feet?

2. A linear function has the table of values below. The information in the table shows the volume of water that flows from a hose in gallons as a function of time in minutes.

Time in Minutes (x)	10	25	50	70
Total Volume of Water in Gallons (y)	44	110	220	308

a. Describe the function in terms of volume and time.

b. Write the rule that represents the linear function that describes the volume of water in gallons, y, in x minutes.

c. What number does the function assign to 250? That is, how many gallons of water flow from the hose in 250 minutes?

d. The average pool has about 17,300 gallons of water. The pool has already been filled $\frac{1}{4}$ of its volume. Write the rule that describes the volume of water flow as a function of time for filling the pool using the hose, including the number of gallons that are already in the pool.

e.   Approximately how much time, in hours, will it take to finish filling the pool?

3.   Recall that a linear function can be described by a rule in the form of $y = mx + b$, where m and b are constants. A particular linear function has the table of values below.

Input (x)	0	4	10	11	15	20	23
Output (y)	4	24	54	59			

a.   What is the equation that describes the function?

b.   Complete the table using the rule.

Lesson Summary

Functions can be described by a rule in the form of $y = mx + b$, where m and b are constants.

Constant rates and proportional relationships can be described by a function, specifically a linear function where the rule is a linear equation.

Functions are described in terms of their inputs and outputs. For example, if the inputs are related to time and the output are distances traveled at given time intervals then we say that the distance traveled is a function of the time spent traveling.

Problem Set

1. A food bank distributes cans of vegetables every Saturday. They keep track of the cans in the following manner in the table. A linear function can be used to represent the data. The information in the table shows the function of time in weeks to the number of cans of vegetables distributed by the food bank.

Number of Weeks (x)	1	12	20	45
Number of Cans of Vegetables Distributed (y)	180	2,160	3,600	8,100

   a. Describe the function in terms of cans distributed and time.

   b. Write the equation or rule that represents the linear function that describes the number of cans handed out, y, in x weeks.

   c. Assume that the food bank wants to distribute 20,000 cans of vegetables. How long will it take them to meet that goal?

   d. Assume that the food bank has already handed out 35,000 cans of vegetables and continues to hand out cans at the same rate each week. Write a linear function that accounts for the number of cans already handed out.

   e. Using your function in part (c), determine how long in years it will take the food bank to hand out 80,000 cans of vegetables.

2. A linear function has the table of values below. The information in the table shows the function of time in hours to the distance an airplane travels in miles. Assume constant speed.

Number of hour traveled (x)	2.5	4	4.2
Distance in miles (y)	1,062.5	1700	1,785

   a. Describe the function in terms of distance and time.

   b. Write the rule that represents the linear function that describes the distance traveled in miles, y, in x hours.

   c. Assume that the airplane is making a trip from New York to Los Angeles which is approximately 2,475 miles. How long will it take the airplane to get to Los Angeles?

   d. The airplane flies for 8 hours. How many miles will it be able to travel in that time interval?

3. A linear function has the table of values below. The information in the table shows the function of time in hours to the distance a car travels in miles.

Number of Hours Traveled (x)	3.5	3.75	4	4.25
Distance in Mmiles (y)	203	217.5	232	246.5

a. Describe the function in terms of area distance and time.

b. Write the rule that represents the linear function that describes the distance traveled in miles, y, in x hours.

c. Assume that the person driving the car is going on a road trip that is 500 miles from their starting point. How long will it take them to get to their destination?

d. Assume that a second car is going on the road trip from the same starting point and traveling at the same rate. However, this car has already driven 210 miles. Write the rule that represents the linear function that accounts for the miles already driven by this car.

e. How long will it take the second car to drive the remainder of the trip?

4. A particular linear function has the table of values below.

Input (x)	2	3	8	11	15	20	23
Output (y)	7	10		34		61	

a. What is the equation that describes the function?

b. Complete the table using the rule.

5. A particular linear function has the table of values below.

Input (x)	0	5	8	13	15	18	21
Output (y)	6	11	14		21		

a. What is the rule that describes the function?

b. Complete the table using the rule.

EUREKA
MATH™

| Lesson 3: | Linear Functions and Proportionality |

Lesson 4: More Examples of Functions

Classwork

Example 1

If 4 copies of the same book cost $256, what is the unit rate for the book?

Example 2

Water flows from a faucet at a constant rate. That is, the volume of water that flows out of the faucet is the same over any given time interval. If 7 gallons of water flow from the faucet every 2 minutes, determine the rule that describes the volume function of the faucet.

Example 3

You have just been served freshly made soup that is so hot that it cannot be eaten. You measure the temperature of the soup, and it is 210°F. Since 212°F is boiling, there is no way it can safely be eaten yet. One minute after receiving the soup the temperature has dropped to 203°F. If you assume that the rate at which the soup cools is linear, write a rule that would describe the rate of cooling of the soup.

Example 4

Consider the following function: There is a function G so that the function assigns to each input, the number of a particular player, an output, their height. For example, the function G assigns to the input, 1 an output of 5'11".

1	5'11"
2	5'4"
3	5'9"
4	5'6"
5	6'3"
6	6'8"
7	5'9"
8	5'10"
9	6'2"

Exercises

1. A linear function has the table of values below related to the number of buses needed for a fieldtrip.

Number of students (x)	35	70	105	140
Number of buses (y)	1	2	3	4

a. Write the linear function that represents the number of buses needed, y, for x number of students.

b. Describe the limitations of x and y.

c. Is the rate discrete or continuous?

d. The entire 8th grade student body of 321 students is going on a fieldtrip. What number of buses does our function assign to 321 students? Explain.

e. Some 7th grade students are going on their own field trip to a different destination, but just 180 are attending. What number does the function assign to 180? How many buses will be needed for the trip?

f. What number does the function assign to 50? Explain what this means and what your answer means.

2. A linear function has the table of values below related to the cost of movie tickets.

Number of tickets (x)	3	6	9	12
Total cost (y)	$27.75	$55.50	$83.25	$111

a. Write the linear function that represents the total cost, y, for x tickets purchased.

b. Is the rate discrete or continuous? Explain.

c. What number does the function assign to 4? What does the question and your answer mean?

Lesson 4:   More Examples of Functions

3.   A function produces the following table of values.

Input	Output
Banana	Yellow
Cherry	Red
Orange	Orange
Tangerine	Orange
Strawberry	Red

a.   Can this function be described by a rule using numbers? Explain.

b.   Describe the assignment of the function.

c.   State an input and the assignment the function would give to its output.

Lesson Summary

Not all functions are linear. In fact, not all functions can be described using numbers.

Linear functions can have discrete rates and continuous rates.

A rate that can have only integer inputs may be used in a function so that it makes sense, and it is then called a **discrete rate**. For example, when planning for a field trip, it only makes sense to plan for a whole number of students and a whole number of buses, not fractional values of either.

Continuous rates are those where any interval, including fractional values, can be used for an input. For example, determining the distance a person walks for a given time interval. The input, which is time in this case, can be in minutes or fractions of minutes.

Problem Set

1. A linear function has the table of values below related to the total cost for gallons of gas purchased.

Number of gallons (x)	5.4	6	15	17
Total cost (y)	$19.71	$21.90	$54.75	$62.05

    a. Write the linear function that represents the total cost, y, for x gallons of gas.

    b. Describe the limitations of x and y.

    c. Is the rate discrete or continuous?

    d. What number does the function assign to 20? Explain what your answer means.

2. A function has the table of values below. Examine the information in the table to answer the questions below.

Input	Output
one	3
two	3
three	5
four	4
five	4
six	3
seven	5

    a. Describe the function.

    b. What number would the function assign to the word "eleven"?

Lesson 4:   More Examples of Functions

3. A linear function has the table of values below related to the total number of miles driven in a given time interval in hours.

Number of hours driven (x)	3	4	5	6
Total miles driven (y)	141	188	235	282

a. Write the linear function that represents the total miles driven, y, for x number of hours.

b. Describe the limitations of x and y.

c. Is the rate discrete or continuous?

d. What number does the function assign to 8? Explain what your answer means.

e. Use the function to determine how much time it would take to drive 500 miles.

4. A function has the table of values below that gives temperatures at specific times over a period of 8 hours.

12:00 p.m.	92°
1:00 p.m.	90.5°
2:00 p.m.	89°
4:00 p.m.	86°
8:00 p.m.	80°

a. Is the function a linear function? Explain.

b. Describe the limitations of x and y.

c. Is the rate discrete or continuous?

d. Let y represent the temperature and x represent the number of hours from 12:00 p.m. Write a rule that describes the function of time on temperature.

e. Check that the rule you wrote to describe the function works for each of the input and output values given in the table.

f. Use the function to determine the temperature at 5:30 p.m.

g. Is it reasonable to assume that this function could be used to predict the temperature for 10:00 a.m. the following day or a temperature at any time on a day next week? Give specific examples in your explanation.

Lesson 5: Graphs of Functions and Equations

Classwork

Exercises

1. The distance that Giselle can run is a function of the amount of time she spends running. Giselle runs 3 miles in 21 minutes. Assume she runs at a constant rate.

    a. Write an equation in two variables that represents her distance ran, y, as a function of the time, x, she spends running.

    b. Use the equation you wrote in part (a) to determine how many miles Giselle can run in 14 minutes.

    c. Use the equation you wrote in part (a) to determine how many miles Giselle can run in 28 minutes.

    d. Use the equation you wrote in part (a) to determine how many miles Giselle can run in 7 minutes.

    e. The input of the function, x, is time and the output of the function, y, is the distance Giselle ran. Write the input and outputs from parts (b)–(d) as ordered pairs and plot them as points on a coordinate plane.

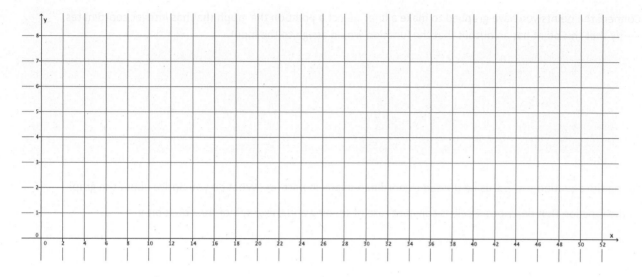

f. What shape does the graph of the points appear to take?

g. Is the rate continuous or discrete?

h. Use the equation you wrote in part (a) to determine how many miles Giselle can run in 36 minutes. Write your answer as an ordered pair as you did in part (e) and include the point on the graph. Is the point in a place where you expected it to be? Explain.

i. Assume you used the rule that describes the function to determine how many miles Giselle can run for any given time and wrote each answer as an ordered pair. Where do you think these points would appear on the graph?

j. What do you think the graph of this function will look like? Explain.

k. Connect the points you have graphed to make a line. Select a point on the graph that has integer coordinates. Verify that this point has an output that the function would assign to the input.

l. Graph the equation $y = \frac{1}{7}x$ using the same coordinate plane in part (e). What do you notice about the graph of the function that describes Giselle's constant rate of running and the graph of the equation $y = \frac{1}{7}x$?

2. Graph the equation $y = x^2$ for positive values of x. Organize your work using the table below, and then answer the questions that follow.

x	y
0	
1	
2	
3	
4	
5	
6	

a. Graph the ordered pairs on the coordinate plane.

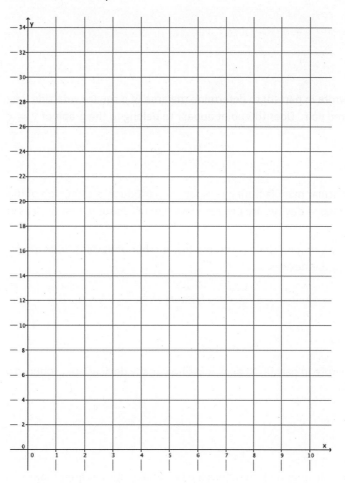

b. What shape does the graph of the points appear to take?

c. Is this equation a linear equation? Explain.

d. An area function has the rule so that it assigns to each input, the length of one side of a square, s, the output, the area of the square, A. Write the rule for this function.

e.   What do you think the graph of this function will look like? Explain.

f.   Use the function you wrote in part (d) to determine the area of a square with side length 2.5. Write the input and output as an ordered pair. Does this point appear to belong to the graph of $y = x^2$?

3.   The number of devices a particular manufacturing company can produce is a function of the number of hours spent making the devices. On average, 4 devices are produced each hour. Assume that devices are produced at a constant rate.

a.   Write an equation in two variables that represents the number of devices, y, as a function of the time the company spends making the devices, x.

b.   Use the equation you wrote in part (a) to determine how many devices are produced in 8 hours.

c.   Use the equation you wrote in part (a) to determine how many devices are produced in 6 hours.

d.   Use the equation you wrote in part (a) to determine how many devices are produced in 4 hours.

e.   The input of the function, x, is time and the output of the function, y, is the number of devices produced. Write the input and outputs from parts (b)–(d) as ordered pairs and plot them as points on a coordinate plane.

EUREKA
MATH™

Lesson 5:   Graphs of Functions and Equations

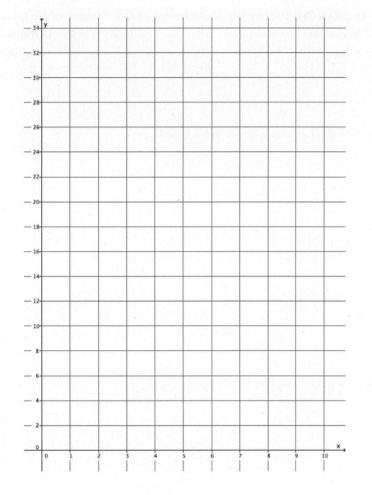

f. What shape does the graph of the points appear to take?

g. Is the rate continuous or discrete?

h. Use the equation you wrote in part (a) to determine how many devices are produced in 1.5 hours. Write your answer as an ordered pair as you did in part (e) and include the point on the graph. Is the point in a place where you expected it to be? Explain.

i. Assume you used the rule that describes the function to determine how many devices are produced for any given time and wrote each answer as an ordered pair. Where do you think these points would appear on the graph?

j. What do you think the graph of this function will look like? Explain.

k. Connect the points you have graphed to make a line. Select a point on the graph that has integer coordinates. Verify that this point has an output that the function would assign to the input.

l. Graph the equation $y = 4x$ using the same coordinate plane in part (e). What do you notice about the graph of the function that describes the company's constant rate of producing devices and the graph of the equation $y = 4x$?

4. Examine the three graphs below. Which, if any, could represent the graph of a function? Explain why or why not for each graph.

Graph 1:

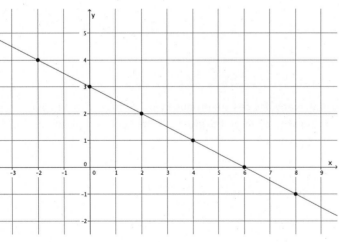

Graph 2:

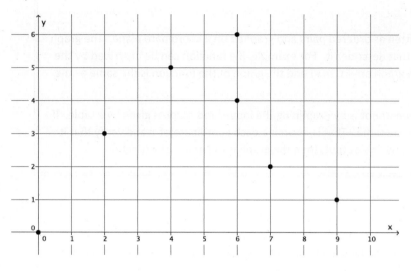

Graph 3:

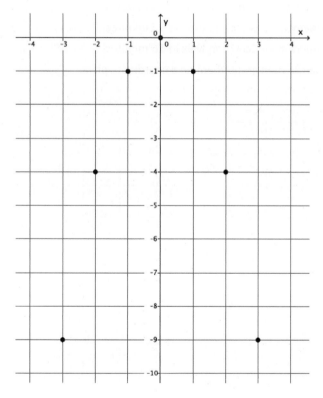

Lesson Summary

The inputs and outputs of a function can be written as ordered pairs and graphed on a coordinate plane. The graph of a function is the same as the rule (equation) that describes it. For example, if a function can be described by the equation $y = mx$, then the ordered pairs of the graph are (x, mx) and the graph of the function is the same as the graph of the equation, $y = mx$.

One way to determine if a set of data is a function or not is by examining the inputs and outputs given by a table. If the data is in the form of a graph, the process is the same. That is, examine each coordinate of x and verify that it has only one y coordinate. If each input has exactly one output, then the graph is the graph of a function.

Problem Set

1. The distance that Scott walks is a function of the time he spends walking. Scott can walk $\frac{1}{2}$ mile every 8 minutes. Assume he walks at a constant rate.

    a. Predict the shape of the graph of the function. Explain.

    b. Write an equation to represent the distance that Scott can walk, y, in x minutes.

    c. Use the equation you wrote in part (b) to determine how many miles Scott can walk in 24 minutes.

    d. Use the equation you wrote in part (a) to determine how many miles Scott can walk in 12 minutes.

    e. Use the equation you wrote in part (a) to determine how many miles Scott can walk in 16 minutes.

    f. Write your inputs and corresponding outputs as ordered pairs. Then graph them on a coordinate plane.

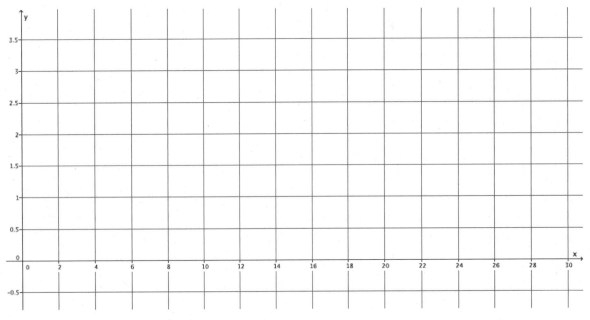

    g. What shape does the graph of the points appear to take? Does it match your prediction?

    h. If the rate of Scott's walking is continuous, connect the points to make a line, and then write the equation that represents the graph of the function. What do you notice?

Lesson 5:   Graphs of Functions and Equations

2. Graph the equation $y = x^3$ for positive values of x. Organize your work using the table below, and then answer the questions that follow.

x	y
0	
0.5	
1	
1.5	
2	
2.5	

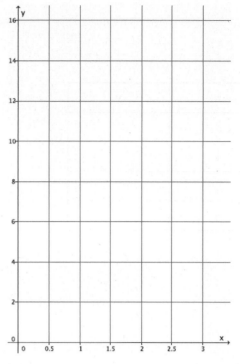

a. Graph the ordered pairs on the coordinate plane.

b. What shape does the graph of the points appear to take?

c. Is this the graph of a linear function? Explain.

d. A volume function has the rule so that it assigns to each input, the length of one side of a cube, s, the output, the volume of the cube, V. The rule for this function is $V = s^3$. What do you think the graph of this function will look like? Explain.

e. Use the function in part (d) to determine the area of a volume with side length of 3. Write the input and output as an ordered pair. Does this point appear to belong to the graph of $y = x^3$?

3. Graph the equation $y = 180(x - 2)$ for whole numbers. Organize your work using the table below, and then answer the questions that follow.

x	y
3	
4	
5	
6	

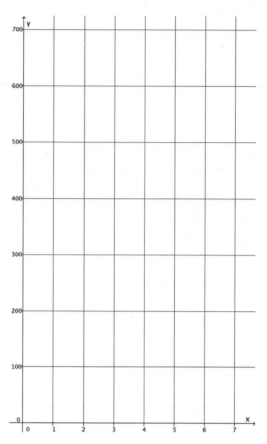

a. Graph the ordered pairs on the coordinate plane.

b. What shape does the graph of the points appear to take?

c. Is this graph a graph of a function? How do you know?

d. Is this a linear equation? Explain.

e. The sum of interior angles of a polygon has the rule so that it assigns each input, the number of sides, n, of the polygon the output, S, the sum of the interior angles of the polygon. The rule for this function is $S = 180(n - 2)$. What do you think the graph of this function will look like? Explain.

f. Is this function continuous or discrete? Explain.

4. Examine the graph below. Could the graph represent the graph of a function? Explain why or why not.

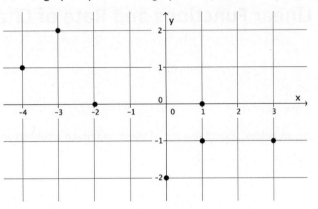

5. Examine the graph below. Could the graph represent the graph of a function? Explain why or why not.

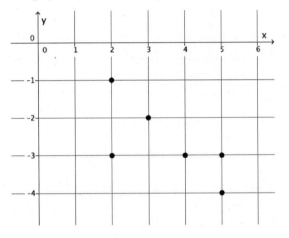

6. Examine the graph below. Could the graph represent the graph of a function? Explain why or why not.

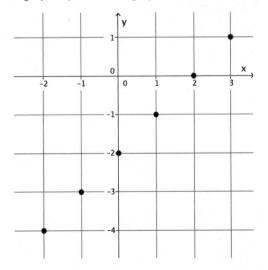

Lesson 6: Graphs of Linear Functions and Rate of Change

Classwork

Opening Exercise

Functions 1, 2, and 3 have the tables shown below. Examine each of them and make a conjecture about which will be linear and justify your claim.

Input	Output
2	5
4	7
5	8
8	11

Input	Output
2	4
3	9
4	16
5	25

Input	Output
0	−3
1	1
2	6
3	9

Exercise

A function assigns the inputs and corresponding outputs shown in the table below.

Input	Output
1	2
2	−1
4	−7
6	−13

a. Is the function a linear function? Check at least three pairs of inputs and their corresponding outputs.

b. What equation describes the function?

c. What will the graph of the function look like? Explain.

Lesson Summary

When the rate of change is constant for pairs of inputs and their corresponding outputs, the function is a linear function.

We can write linear equations in the form of $y = mx + b$ to express a linear function.

From the last lesson we know that the graph of a function is the same as the graph of the equation that describes it. When a function can be described by the linear equation $y = mx + b$, the graph of the function will be a line because the graph of the equation $y = mx + b$ is a line.

Problem Set

1. A function assigns the inputs and corresponding outputs shown in the table below.

Input	Output
3	9
9	17
12	21
15	25

   a. Is the function a linear function? Check at least three pairs of inputs and their corresponding outputs.

   b. What equation describes the function?

   c. What will the graph of the function look like? Explain.

2. A function assigns the inputs and corresponding outputs shown in the table below.

Input	Output
−1	2
0	0
1	2
2	8
3	18

   a. Is the function a linear function?

   b. What equation describes the function?

3. A function assigns the inputs and corresponding outputs shown in the table below.

Input	Output
0.2	2
0.6	6
1.5	15
2.1	21

   a. Is the function a linear function? Check at least three pairs of inputs and their corresponding outputs.

   b. What equation describes the function?

   c. What will the graph of the function look like? Explain.

Lesson 6:   Graphs of Linear Functions and Rate of Change

4. Martin says that you only need to check the first and last input and output values to determine if the function is linear. Is he correct? Explain. Hint: Show an example with a table that is not a function.

5. Is the following graph a graph of a linear function? How would you determine if it is a linear function?

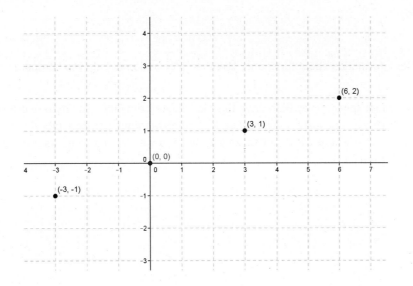

6. A function assigns the inputs and corresponding outputs shown in the table below.

Input	Output
−6	−6
−5	−5
−4	−4
−2	−2

a. Is the function a linear function? Check at least three pairs of inputs and their corresponding outputs.

b. What equation describes the function?

c. What will the graph of the function look like? Explain.

Lesson 7: Comparing Linear Functions and Graphs

Classwork

Exercises

Each of the Exercises 1–4 provides information about functions. Use that information to help you compare the functions and answer the question.

1. Alan and Margot drive at a constant speed. They both drive the same route from City A to City B, a distance of 147 miles. Alan begins driving at 1:40 p.m. and arrives at City B at 4:15 p.m. Margot's trip from City A to City B can be described with the equation $y = 64x$, where y is the distance traveled and x is the time in hours spent traveling. Who gets from City A to City B faster?

2. You have recently begun researching phone billing plans. Phone Company A charges a flat rate of $75 a month. A flat rate means that your bill will be $75 each month with no additional costs. The billing plan for Phone Company B is a function of the number of texts that you send that month. That is, the total cost of the bill changes each month depending on how many texts you send. The table below represents the inputs and the corresponding outputs that the function assigns.

Input (number of texts)	Output (cost of bill)
50	$50
150	$60
200	$65
500	$95

At what number of texts would the bill from each phone plan be the same? At what number of texts is Phone Company A the better choice? At what number of texts is Phone Company B the better choice?

3. A function describes the volume of water in gallons, y, that flows from faucet A for x minutes. The graph below is the graph of this function. Faucet B's water flow can be described by the equation $y = \frac{5}{6}x$, where y is the volume of water in gallons that flows from the faucet in x minutes. Assume the flow of water from each faucet is constant. Which faucet has a faster flow of water? Each faucet is being used to fill tubs with a volume of 50 gallons. How long will it take each faucet to fill the tub? How do you know? The tub that is filled by faucet A already has 15 gallons in it. If both faucets are turned on at the same time, which faucet will fill its tub faster?

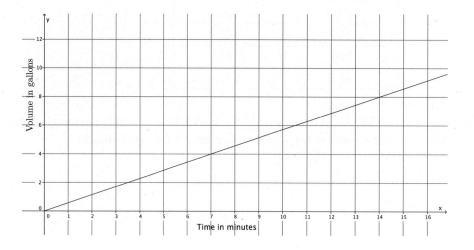

4. Two people, Adam and Bianca, are competing to see who can save the most money in one month. Use the table and the graph below to determine who will save more money at the end of the month. State how much money each person had at the start of the competition.

Adam's Savings: Bianca's Savings:

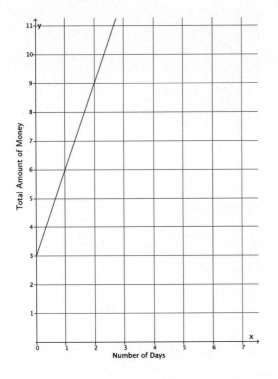

Input (Number of Days)	Output (Total amount of money)
5	$17
8	$26
12	$38
20	$62

Problem Set

1. The graph below represents the distance, y, Car A travels in x minutes. The table represents the distance, y, Car B travels in x minutes. Which car is traveling at a greater speed? How do you know?

    Car A:

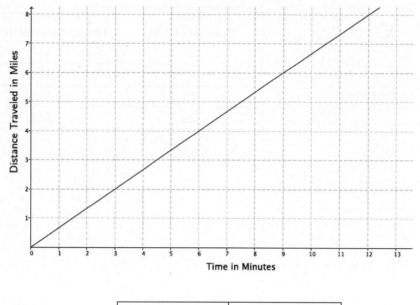

    Car B:

Time in minutes (x)	Distance (y)
15	12.5
30	25
45	37.5

2. The local park needs to replace an existing fence that is six feet high. Fence Company A charges $7,000 for building materials and $200 per foot for the length of the fence. Fence Company B charges based on the length of the fence. That is, the total cost of the six foot high fence will depend on how long the fence is. The table below represents the inputs and the corresponding outputs that the function assigns for Fence Company B.

Input (length of fence)	Output (cost of bill)
100	$26,000
120	$31,200
180	$46,800
250	$65,000

    a. Which company charges a higher rate per foot of fencing? How do you know?

    b. At what number of the length of the fence would the cost from each fence company be the same? What will the cost be when the companies charge the same amount? If the fence you need is 190 feet in length, which company would be a better choice?

3. The rule $y = 123x$ is used to describe the function for the number of minutes needed x to produce y toys at Toys Plus. Another company, #1 Toys, has a similar function that assigned the values shown in the table below. Which company produces toys at a slower rate? Explain.

Time in minutes (x)	Toys Produced (y)
5	600
11	1,320
13	1,560

4. A function describes the number of miles a train can travel, y, for the number of hours, x. The graph below is the graph of this function. Assume constant speed. The train is traveling from City A to City B (a distance of 320 miles). After 4 hours, the train slows down to a constant speed of 48 miles per hour.

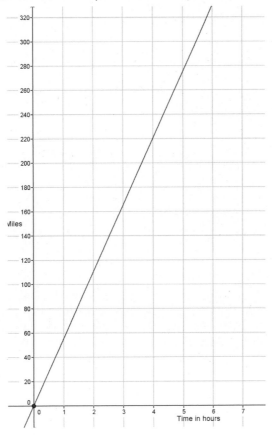

a. How long will it take the train to reach its destination?

b. If the train had not slowed down after 4 hours, how long would it have taken to reach its destination?

c. Suppose after 4 hours, the train increased its constant speed. How fast would the train have to travel to complete the destination in 1.5 hours?

Lesson 7: Comparing Linear Functions and Graphs

5. a. A hose is used to fill up a 1,200 gallon water truck at a constant rate. After 10 minutes, there are 65 gallons of water in the truck. After 15 minutes, there are 82 gallons of water in the truck. How long will it take to fill up the water truck?

    b. The driver of the truck realizes that something is wrong with the hose he is using. After 30 minutes, he shuts off the hose and tries a different hose. The second hose has a constant rate of 18 gallons per minute. How long does it take the second hose to fill up the truck?

    c. Could there ever be a time when the first hose and the second hose filled up the same amount of water?

Lesson 8: Graphs of Simple Non-Linear Functions

Classwork

Exercises

1. A function has the rule so that each input of x is assigned an output of x^2.

    a. Do you think the function is linear or non-linear? Explain.

    b. Develop a list of inputs and outputs for this function. Organize your work using the table below. Then, answer the questions that follow.

Input (x)	Output (x^2)
−5	
−4	
−3	
−2	
−1	
0	
1	
2	
3	
4	
5	

    c. Graph the inputs and outputs as points on the coordinate plane where the output is the y-coordinate.

d.   What shape does the graph of the points appear to take?

e.   Find the rate of change using rows 1 and 2 from the table above.

f.   Find the rate of change using rows 2 and 3 from the above table.

g.   Find the rate of change using any two other rows from the above table.

h.   Return to your initial claim about the function. Is it linear or non-linear? Justify your answer with as many pieces of evidence as possible.

2.   A function has the rule so that each input of x is assigned an output of x^3.

a.   Do you think the function is linear or non-linear? Explain.

b. Develop a list of inputs and outputs for this function. Organize your work using the table below. Then, answer the questions that follow.

Input (x)	Output (x^3)
-2.5	
-2	
-1.5	
-1	
-0.5	
0	
0.5	
1	
1.5	
2	
2.5	

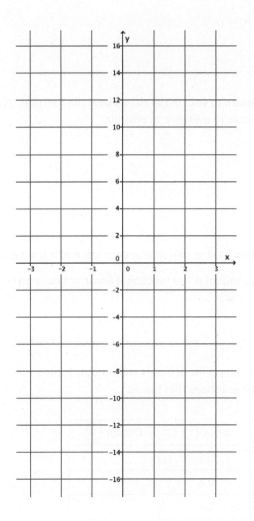

c. Graph the inputs and outputs as points on the coordinate plane where the output is the y-coordinate.

d. What shape does the graph of the points appear to take?

e. Find the rate of change using rows 2 and 3 from the table above.

f. Find the rate of change using rows 3 and 4 from the table above.

g. Find the rate of change using rows 8 and 9 from the table above.

h. Return to your initial claim about the function. Is it linear or non-linear? Justify your answer with as many
    pieces of evidence as possible.

3. A function has the rule so that each input of x is assigned an output of $\dfrac{1}{x}$ for values of $x > 0$.

    a. Do you think the function is linear or non-linear? Explain.

    b. Develop a list of inputs and outputs for this function. Organize your work using the table below. Then, answer
        the questions that follow.

Input (x)	Output $\left(\dfrac{1}{x}\right)$
0.1	
0.2	
0.4	
0.5	
0.8	
1	
1.6	
2	
2.5	
4	
5	

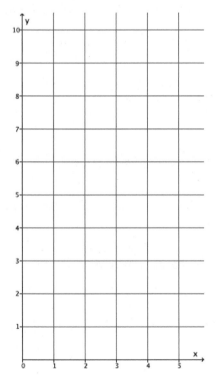

    c. Graph the inputs and outputs as points on the coordinate
        plane where the output is the y-coordinate.

d.   What shape does the graph of the points appear to take?

e.   Find the rate of change using rows 1 and 2 from the table above.

f.   Find the rate of change using rows 2 and 3 from the table above.

g.   Find the rate of change using any two other rows from the table above.

h.   Return to your initial claim about the function. Is it linear or non-linear? Justify your answer with as many
     pieces of evidence as possible.

In Exercises 4–10 the rule that describes a function is given. If necessary, use a table to organize pairs of inputs and
outputs, and then graph each on a coordinate plane to help answer the questions.

4.   What shape do you expect the graph of the function described by $y = x$ to take? Is it a linear or non-linear
     function?

5. What shape do you expect the graph of the function described by $y = 2x^2 - x$ to take? Is it a linear or non-linear function?

6. What shape do you expect the graph of the function described by $3x + 7y = 8$ to take? Is it a linear or non-linear function?

7. What shape do you expect the graph of the function described by $y = 4x^3$ to take? Is it a linear or non-linear function?

8. What shape do you expect the graph of the function described by $\frac{3}{x} = y$ to take? Is it a linear or non-linear function?

9. What shape do you expect the graph of the function described by $\frac{4}{x^2} = y$ to take? Is it a linear or non-linear function?

10. What shape do you expect the graph of the equation $x^2 + y^2 = 36$ to take? Is it a linear or non-linear? Is it a function? Explain.

Lesson Summary

One way to determine if a function is linear or non-linear is by inspecting the rate of change using a table of values or by examining its graph. Functions described by non-linear equations do not have a constant rate of change. Because some functions can be described by equations, an examination of the equation allows you to determine if the function is linear or non-linear. Just like with equations, when the exponent of the variable x is not equal to 1, then the equation is non-linear; therefore, the function described by a non-linear equation will graph as some kind of curve, i.e., not a line.

Problem Set

1. A function has the rule so that each input of x is assigned an output of $x^2 - 4$.

    a. Do you think the function is linear or non-linear? Explain.

    b. What shape do you expect the graph of the function to be?

    c. Develop a list of inputs and outputs for this function. Graph the input and outputs as points on the coordinate plane where the output is the y-coordinate.

    d. Was your prediction correct?

Input (x)	Output $(x^2 - 4)$
-3	
-2	
-1	
0	
1	
2	
3	

2. A function has the rule so that each input of x is assigned an output of $\dfrac{1}{x+3}$.

    a. Is the function linear or non-linear? Explain.

    b. What shape do you expect the graph of the function to take?

    c. Given the inputs in the table below, use the rule of the function to determine the corresponding outputs. Graph the inputs and outputs as points on the coordinate plane where the output is the y-coordinate.

    d. Was your prediction correct?

Input (x)	Output $\left(\dfrac{1}{x+3}\right)$
-2	
-1	
0	
1	
2	
3	

3. Is the function that is represented by this graph linear or non-linear? Explain. Show work that supports your claim.

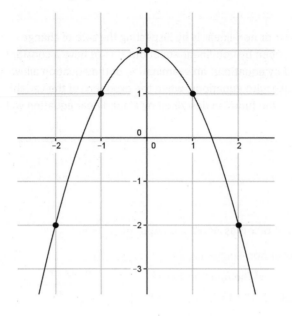

Lesson 9: Examples of Functions from Geometry

Classwork

Exercises

As you complete Exercises 1–4, record the information in the table below.

	Side length (s)	Area (A)	Expression that describes area of border
Exercise 1			
Exercise 2			
Exercise 3			
Exercise 4			

1.   Use the figure below to answer parts (a)–(f).

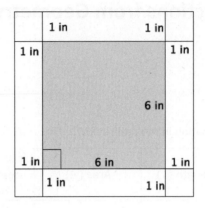

a.   What is the length of one side of the smaller, inner square?

b.   What is the area of the smaller, inner square?

c.   What is the length of one side of the larger, outer square?

d.   What is the area of the area of the larger, outer square?

e.   Use your answers in parts (b) and (d) to determine the area of the 1-inch white border of the figure.

f.   Explain your strategy for finding the area of the white border.

2. Use the figure below to answer parts (a)–(f).

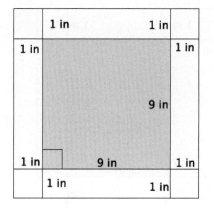

a. What is the length of one side of the smaller, inner square?

b. What is the area of the smaller, inner square?

c. What is the length of one side of the larger, outer square?

d. What is the area of the area of the larger, outer square?

e. Use your answers in parts (b) and (d) to determine the area of the 1-inch white border of the figure.

f. Explain your strategy for finding the area of the white border.

3. Use the figure below to answer parts (a)–(f).

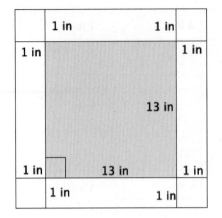

a. What is the length of one side of the smaller, inner square?

b. What is the area of the smaller, inner square?

c. What is the length of one side of the larger, outer square?

d. What is the area of the area of the larger, outer square?

e. Use your answers in parts (b) and (d) to determine the area of the 1-inch white border of the figure.

f. Explain your strategy for finding the area of the white border.

4. Write a function that would allow you to calculate the area of a 1-inch white border for any sized square picture measured in inches.

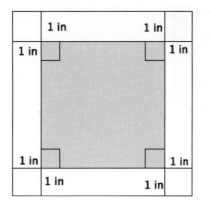

a. Write an expression that represents the side length of the smaller, inner square.

b. Write an expression that represents the area of the smaller, inner square.

c. Write an expression that represents the side lengths of the larger, outer square.

d. Write an expression that represents the area of the larger, outer square.

e. Use your expressions in parts (b) and (d) to write a function for the area A of the 1-inch white border for any sized square picture measured in inches.

5. The volume of the prism shown below is 61.6 in^3. What is the height of the prism?

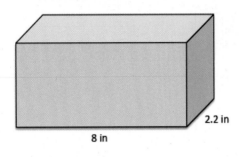

2.2 in

8 in

6. Find the value of the ratio that compares the volume of the larger prism to the smaller prism.

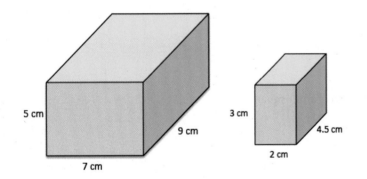

5 cm

9 cm

7 cm

3 cm

4.5 cm

2 cm

As you complete Exercises 7–10, record the information in the table below.

	Area of base (A)	Height (h)	Volume
Exercise 7			
Exercise 8			
Exercise 9			
Exercise 10			

7. Use the figure below to answer parts (a)–(c).

    a. What is the area of the base?

    b. What is the height of the figure?

    c. What is the volume of the figure?

3 cm

3 cm

12 cm

8. Use the figure to the right to answer parts (a)–(c).

    a. What is the area of the base?

    b. What is the height of the figure?

    c. What is the volume of the figure?

8 cm

3 cm

12 cm

9. Use the figure to the right to answer parts (a)–(c).
    a.   What is the area of the base?

    b.   What is the height of the figure?

    c.   What is the volume of the figure?

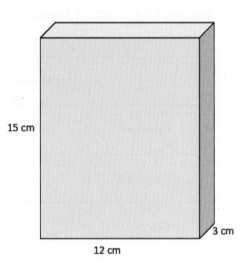

15 cm

3 cm

12 cm

10. Use the figure to the right to answer parts (a)–(c).
    a.   What is the area of the base?

    b.   What is the height of the figure?

    c.   Write and describe a function that will allow you to
         determine the volume of any rectangular prism that has a
         base area of 36 cm^2.

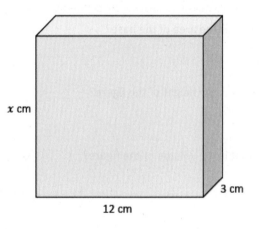

x cm

3 cm

12 cm

Problem Set

1. Calculate the area of the 3-inch white border of the square figure below.

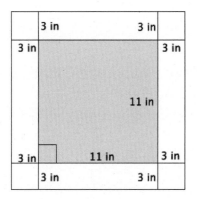

2. Write a function that would allow you to calculate the area A of a 3-inch white border for any sized square picture measured in inches.

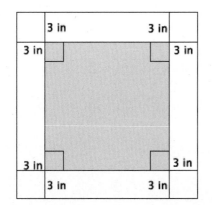

3. Dartboards typically have an outer ring of numbers that represent the number of points a player can score for getting a dart in that section. A simplified dartboard is shown below. The center of the circle is point A. Calculate the area of the outer ring. Write an exact answer that uses π (do not approximate your answer by using 3.14 for π).

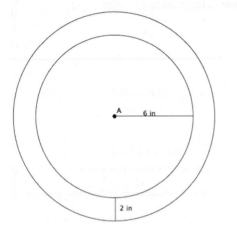

4. Write a function that would allow you to calculate the area A of the outer ring for any sized dartboard with radius r. Write an exact answer that uses π (do not approximate your answer by using 3.14 for π).

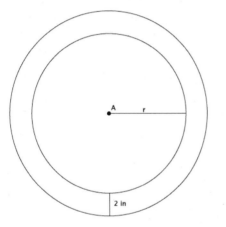

5. The solid shown was filled with water and then poured into the standard rectangular prism as shown. The height that the volume reaches is 14.2 in. What is the volume of the solid?

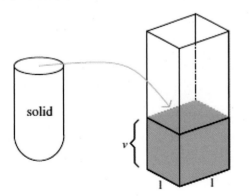

6. Determine the volume of the rectangular prism shown below.

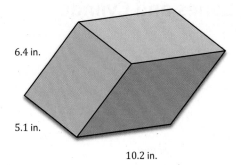

6.4 in.

5.1 in.

10.2 in.

7. The volume of the prism shown below is 972 cm³. What is its length?

8.1 cm

5 cm

8. The volume of the prism shown below is 32.7375 ft³. What is its width?

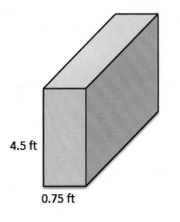

4.5 ft

0.75 ft

9. Determine the volume of the 3-dimensional figure below. Explain how you got your answer.

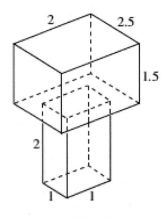

2   2.5

1.5

2

1   1

Lesson 10: Volumes of Familiar Solids—Cones and Cylinders

Exercises

1.

    a.   Write an equation to determine the volume of the rectangular prism shown below.

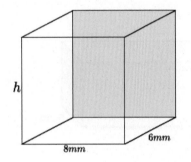

    b.   Write an equation to determine the volume of the rectangular prism shown below.

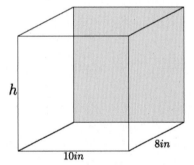

    c.   Write an equation to determine the volume of the rectangular prism shown below.

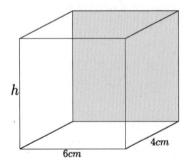

    d.   Write an equation for volume, V, in terms of the area of the base, B.

2. Using what you learned in Exercise 1, write an equation to determine the volume of the cylinder shown below.

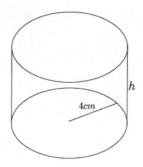

3. Use the diagram at right to answer the questions.
   a. What is the area of the base?

   b. What is the height?

   c. What is the volume of the rectangular prism?

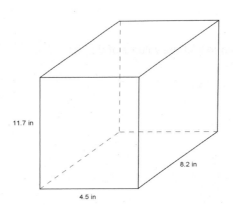

4. Use the diagram at right to answer the questions.
   a. What is the area of the base?

   b. What is the height?

   c. What is the volume of the right cylinder?

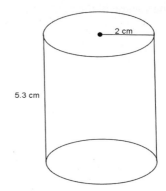

5. Use the diagram at right to answer the questions.

   a. What is the area of the base?

   b. What is the height?

   c. What is the volume of the right cylinder?

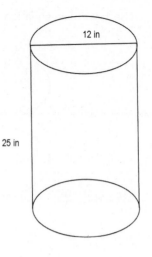

6. Use the diagram to find the volume of the right cone.

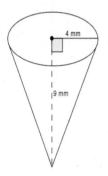

7. Use the diagram to find the volume of the right cone.

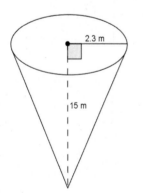

8. Challenge: A container in the shape of a right circular cone has height h, and base of radius r as shown. It is filled with water (in its upright position) to half the height. Assume that the surface of the water is parallel to the base of the inverted cone. Use the diagram to answer the following questions:

a.   What do we know about the lengths of AB and AO?

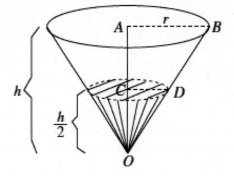

b.   What do we know about the measure of $\angle OAB$ and $\angle OCD$?

c.   What can you say about $\triangle OAB$ and $\triangle OCD$?

d.   What is the ratio of the volume of water to the volume of the container itself?

Lesson Summary

The formula to find the volume V, of a right cylinder is $V = \pi r^2 h = Bh$, where B is the area of the base.

The formula to find the volume of a cone is directly related to that of the cylinder. Given a cylinder with radius r and height h, the volume of a cone with those same dimensions is exaclty one-third of the cylinder. The formula for the volume V, of a cone is $V = \frac{1}{3}\pi r^2 h = \frac{1}{3}Bh$, where B is the area of the base.

Problem Set

1. Use the diagram to help you find the volume of the right cylinder.

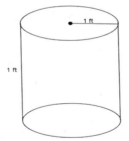

2. Use the diagram to help you find the volume of the right cone.

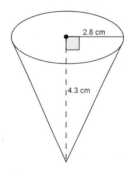

3. Use the diagram to help you find the volume of the right cylinder.

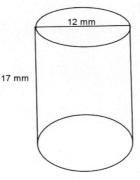

12 mm

17 mm

4. Use the diagram to help you find the volume of the right cone.

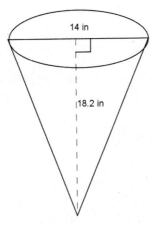

14 in

18.2 in

5. Oscar wants to fill with water a bucket that is the shape of a right cylinder. It has a 6-inch radius and 12-inch height. He uses a shovel that has the shape of right cone with a 3-inch radius and 4-inch height. How many shovelfuls will it take Oscar to fill the bucket up level with the top?

6. A cylindrical tank (with dimensions shown below) contains water that is 1-foot deep. If water is poured into the tank at a constant rate of 20 $\frac{ft^3}{min}$ for 20 min., will the tank overflow? Use 3.14 to estimate π.

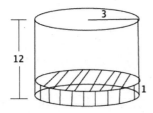

3

12

1

Lesson 11: Volume of a Sphere

Classwork

Exercises 1–3

1. What is the volume of a cylinder?

2. What is the height of the cylinder?

3. If $volume(sphere) = \frac{2}{3} volume(cylinder\ with\ same\ diameter\ and\ height)$, what is the formula for the volume of a sphere?

Example 1

Compute the exact volume for the sphere shown below.

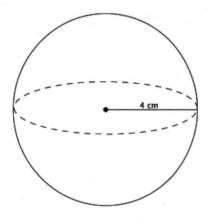

Example 2

A cylinder has a diameter of 16 inches and a height of 14 inches. What is the volume of the largest sphere that will fit into the cylinder?

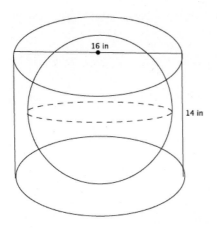

Exercises4–8

4. Use the diagram and the general formula to find the volume of the sphere.

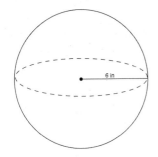

5. The average basketball has a diameter of 9.5 inches. What is the volume of an average basketball? Round your answer to the tenths place.

6. A spherical fish tank has a radius of 8 inches. Assuming the entire tank could be filled with water, what would the volume of the tank be? Round your answer to the tenths place.

7. Use the diagram to answer the questions.

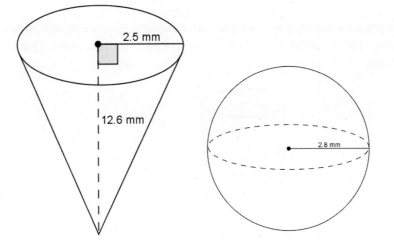

2.5 mm

12.6 mm

2.8 mm

a. Predict which of the figures below has the greater volume. Explain.

b. Use the diagram to find the volume of each and determine which has the larger volume.

8. One of two half spheres formed by a plane through the spheres center is called a hemisphere. What is the formula for the volume of a hemisphere?

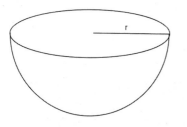

r

Lesson Summary

The formula to find the volume of a sphere is directly related to that of the right circular cylinder. Given a right circular cylinder with radius r and height h, which is equal to $2r$, a sphere with the same radius r has a volume that is exactly two-thirds of the cylinder.

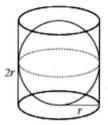

Therefore, the volume of a sphere with radius r has a volume given by the formula $V = \frac{4}{3}\pi r^3$.

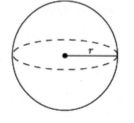

Problem Set

1. Use the diagram to find the volume of the sphere.

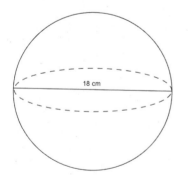

18 cm

2. Determine the volume of a sphere with diameter 9 mm, shown below.

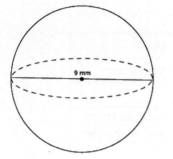

3. Determine the volume of a sphere with diameter 22 in., shown below.

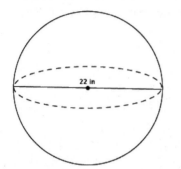

4. Which of the two figures below has the lesser volume?

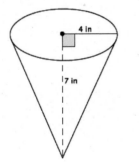 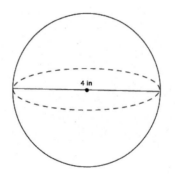

5. Which of the two figures below has the greater volume?

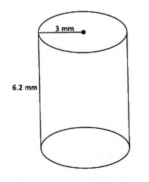 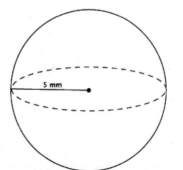

6. Bridget wants to determine which ice cream option is the best choice. The chart below gives the description and prices for her options. Use the space below each item to record your findings.

$2.00	$3.00	$4.00
1 scoop in a cup	2 scoops in a cup	3 scoops in a cup
Half a scoop on a cone filled with ice cream		A cup filled with ice cream (level to the top of the cup)

A scoop of ice cream is considered a perfect sphere and has a 2-inch diameter. A cone has a 2-inch diameter and a height of 4.5 inches. A cup is considered a right circular cylinder, has a 3-inch diameter, and a height of 2 inches.

a. Determine the volume of each choice. Use 3.14 to approximate π.

b. Determine which choice is the best value for her money. Explain your reasoning.

Mathematics Curriculum

π

Copy Ready Material

Name _____   Date _____

Lesson 1: The Concept of a Function

Exit Ticket

1.   A ball bounces across the schoolyard. It hits the ground at $(0,0)$ and bounces up and lands at $(1,0)$ and bounces again. The graph shows only one bounce.

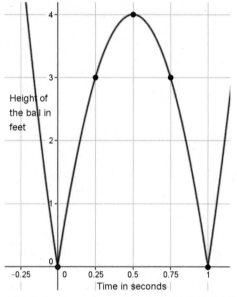

a.   Identify the height of the ball at the following values of t: 0, 0.25, 0.5, 0.75, 1.

b.   What is the average speed of the ball over the first 0.25 seconds? What is the average speed of the ball over the next 0.25 seconds (from 0.25 to 0.5 seconds)?

c.   Is the height of the ball changing at a constant rate?

Name _____   Date _____

Lesson 2: Formal Definition of a Function

Exit Ticket

1. Can the table shown below represent a function? Explain.

Input (x)	10	20	30	40	50
Output (y)	32	64	96	64	32

2. Kelly can tune up four cars in three hours. If we assume he works at a constant rate, we can describe the situation using a function.

   a. Write the rule that describes the function that represents Kelly's constant rate of work.

   b. Use the function you wrote in part (a) as the formula for the function to complete the table below. Round your answers to the hundredths place.

Time it takes to tune up cars (x)	2	3	4	6	7
Number of cars tuned up (y)					

   c. Kelly works 8 hours per day. How many cars will he finish tuning up at the end of a shift?

   d. For this problem we assumed that Kelly worked at a constant rate. Do you think that is a reasonable assumption for this situation? Explain.

Lesson 2:   Formal Definition of a Function

2

Name _____   Date _____

Lesson 3: Linear Functions and Proportionality

Exit Ticket

1. A linear function has the table of values below. The information in the tables shows the number of pages a student can read in a certain book as a function of time in minutes. Assume a constant rate.

Time in Minutes (x)	2	6	11	20
Total Number of Pages Read in a Certain Book (y)	7	21	38.5	70

a. Write the rule or equation that represents the linear function that describes the total number of pages read, y, in x minutes.

b. How many pages can be read in 45 minutes?

c. This certain book has 396 pages. The student has already read $\frac{3}{8}$ of the pages. Write the equation that describes the number of pages read as a function of time for reading this book, including the number pages that have already been read.

d. Approximately how much time, in minutes, will it take to finish reading the book?

Lesson 3:   Linear Functions and Proportionality

Name _____   Date _____

Lesson 4: More Examples of Functions

Exit Ticket

1. A linear function has the table of values below related to the cost of a certain tablet.

Number of tablets (x)	17	22	25
Total cost (y)	$10,183	$13,178	$14,975

a.   Write the linear function that represents the total cost, y, for x number of tablets.

b.   Is the rate discrete or continuous? Explain.

c.   What number does the function assign to 7? Explain.

2. A function produces the following table of values.

Serious	Adjective
Student	Noun
Work	Verb
They	Pronoun
And	Conjunction
Accurately	Adverb

a.   Describe the function.

b.   What part of speech would the function assign to the word continuous?

Name _____   Date _____

Lesson 5: Graphs of Functions and Equations

Exit Ticket

1. The amount of water in gallons that flows out a certain hose is a function of the amount of time the faucet is turned on. The amount of water that flows out of the hose in four minutes is eleven gallons. Assume water flows at a constant rate.

    a. Write an equation in two variables that represents the amount in gallons of water, y, as a function of the time, x, the faucet is turned on.

    b. Use the equation you wrote in part (a) to determine the amount of water that flows out of a hose in 8 minutes, 4 minutes, and 2 minutes.

    c. The input of the function, x, is time and the output of the function, y, is the amount of water that flows out of the hose in gallons. Write the input and outputs from part (b) as ordered pairs and plot them as points on a coordinate plane.

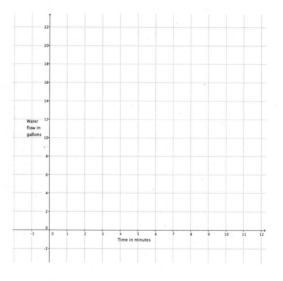

Name _____   Date _____

Lesson 8: Graphs of Simple Non-Linear Functions

Exit Ticket

1. The graph below is the graph of a function. Do you think the function is linear or non-linear? Show work in your explanation that supports your answer.

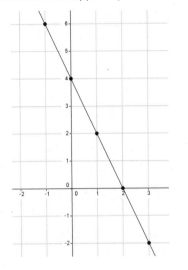

2. A function has the rule so that each input of x is assigned an output of $\frac{1}{2}x^2$. Do you think the graph of the function will be linear or non-linear? What shape do you expect the graph to take? Explain.

Name _____   Date _____

Lesson 9: Examples of Functions from Geometry

Exit Ticket

1. Write a function that would allow you to calculate the area, A, of a 2-inch white border for any sized square figure with sides of length s measured in inches.

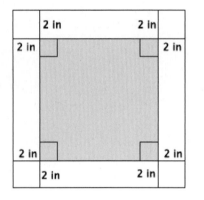

2. The volume of the rectangular prism is 295.68 in^3. What is its width?

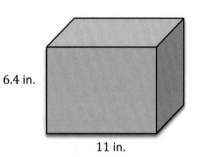

6.4 in.

11 in.

Name _____   Date _____

Lesson 10: Volumes of Familiar Solids – Cones and Cylinders

Exit Ticket

1. Use the diagram to find the total volume of the three cones shown below.

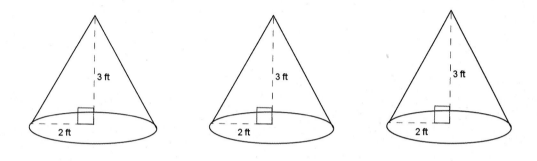

2. Use the diagram below to determine which has the greater volume, the cone or the cylinder?

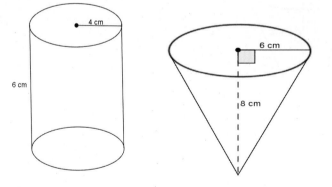

Name _____   Date _____

Lesson 11: Volume of a Sphere

1. What is the volume of the sphere shown below?

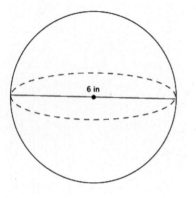

2. Which of the two figures below has the greater volume?

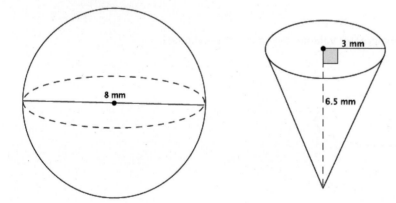

Name _____   Date _____

1.

a. We define x as a year between 2008 and 2013, and y as the total number of smartphones sold that year, in millions. The table shows values of x, and corresponding y values.

Year (x)	2008	2009	2010	2011	2012	2013
Number of smartphones in millions (y)	3.7	17.3	42.4	90	125	153.2

i. How many smartphones were sold in 2009?

ii. In which year were 90 million smartphones sold?

iii. Is y a function of x? Explain why or why not.

b. Randy began completing the table below to represent a particular linear function. Write an equation to represent the function he used, and complete the table for him.

Input (x)	−3	−1	0	$\frac{1}{2}$	1	2	3
Output (y)	−5		4				13

c.   Create the graph of the function in part (b).

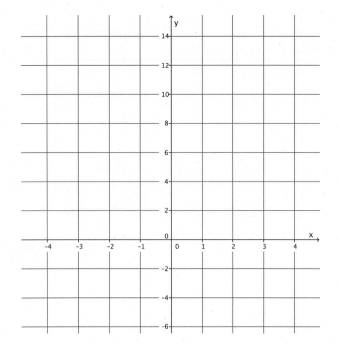

d.   At NYU in 2013, the cost of the weekly meal plan options could be described as a function of the number of meals. Is the cost of the meal plan a linear or non-linear function? Explain.

8 meals: $125/week
10 meals: $135/week
12 meals: $155/week
21 meals: $220/week

2. The cost to enter and go on rides at a local water park, Wally's Water World, is shown in the graph below.

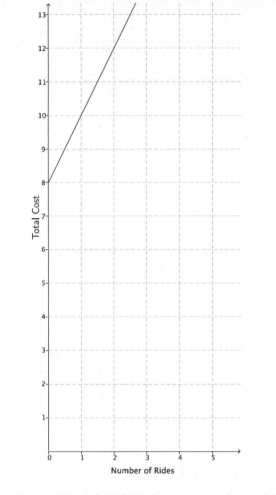

Number of Rides

A new water park just opened named Tony's Tidal Takeover. You haven't heard anything specific about how much it costs to go to this park, but some of your friends have told you what they spent. The information is organized in the table below.

# of rides	0	2	4	6
$ spent	12	13.50	15	16.50

Each park charges a different admission fee and a different fee per ride, but the cost of each ride remains the same.

a. If you only have $14 to spend, which park would you attend (assume the rides are the same quality)? Explain.

b. Another water park, Splash, opens and they charge an admission fee of $30 with no additional fee for rides. At what number of rides does it become more expensive to go to Wally's Water Park than Splash? At what number of rides does it become more expensive to go to Tony's Tidal Takeover than Splash?

c. For all three water parks, the cost is a function of the number of rides. Compare the functions for all three water parks in terms of their rate of change. Describe the impact it has on the total cost of attending each park.

3. For each part below, leave your answers in terms of π.
    a. Determine the volume for each three-dimensional figure shown below.

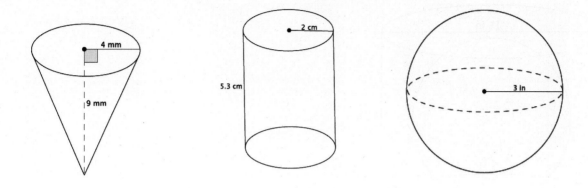

    b. You want to fill the cylinder shown below with water. All you have is a container shaped like a cone
        with a radius of 3 inches and a height of 5 inches; you can use this cone-shaped container to take
        water from a faucet and fill the cylinder. How many cones will it take to fill the cylinder?

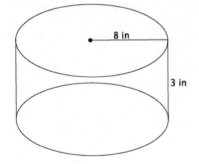

c.   You have a cylinder with a diameter of 15 inches and height of 12 inches. What is the volume of the largest sphere that will fit inside of it?

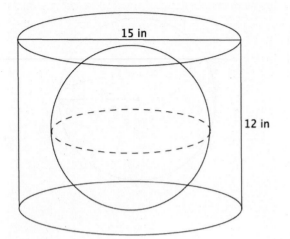

Staff

Nashrah Ahmed, Coordinator of User Experience
Deirdre Bey, Formatter
Thomas Brasdefer, Formatter
Brenda Bryant, Program Operations Associate
Adrienne Burgess, Project Associate – Website Content
Alyson Burgess, Associate Director of Administration
Rose Calloway, Document Specialist
Adam Cardais, Copy Editor
Jamie Carruth, Formatter
Lauren Chapalee, Professional Learning Manager – English
Gregar Chapin, Website Project Coordinator
Chris Clary, Director of Branding and Marketing
Katelyn Colacino, Formatter
Julia Cooper, Formatter
Barbara Davidson, Deputy Director
Karen Elkins, Formatter
Jennifer George, Formatter
Erin Glover, Formatter
Laurie Gonsoulin, Formatter
Eric Halley, Formatter
Candice Hartley, Formatter
Thomas Haynes, Copy Editor
Robert Hunsicker, Program Operations Associate
Jennifer Hutchinson, Copy Editor
Anne Ireland, Print Edition Coordinator

Maggie Kay, Copy Editor
Liz LeBarron, Program Operations and Support Associate
Jeff LeBel, XML Developer
Tam Le, Document Production Manager
Natanya Levioff, Director of Program Operations and Support
Siena Mazero, Project Associate – Website Content
Stacie McClintock, XML Developer
Cindy Medici, Copy Editor
Elisabeth Mox, Executive Assistant to the President
Lynne Munson, President and Executive Director
Sarah Oyler, Document Specialist
Diego Quiroga, Accounts Specialist
Becky Robinson, Program Operations Associate
Amy Rome, Copy Editor
Rachel Rooney, Program Manager – English/History
Neela Roy, Print Edition Associate
Tim Shen, Customer Relations Associate
Kathleen Smith, Formatter
Leigh Sterten, Project Associate – Web Content
Wendy Taylor, Copy Editor
Megan Wall, Formatter
Marjani Warren, Account Manager
Sam Wertheim, Product Delivery Manager
Amy Wierzbicki, Assets and Permissions Manager
Sarah Woodard, Associate Director – English/History

Eureka Math: A Story of Ratios **Contributors**

Michael Allwood, Curriculum Writer

Tiah Alphonso, Program Manager – Curriculum Production

Catriona Anderson, Program Manager – Implementation Support

Beau Bailey, Curriculum Writer

Scott Baldridge, Lead Mathematician and Lead Curriculum Writer

Bonnie Bergstresser, Math Auditor

Gail Burrill, Curriculum Writer

Beth Chance, Statistician

Joanne Choi, Curriculum Writer

Jill Diniz, Program Director

Lori Fanning, Curriculum Writer

Ellen Fort, Math Auditor

Kathy Fritz, Curriculum Writer

Glenn Gebhard, Curriculum Writer

Krysta Gibbs, Curriculum Writer

Winnie Gilbert, Lead Curriculum Writer / Editor, Grade 8

Pam Goodner, Math Auditor

Debby Grawn, Curriculum Writer

Bonnie Hart, Curriculum Writer

Stefanie Hassan, Lead Curriculum Writer / Editor, Grade 8

Sherri Hernandez, Math Auditor

Patrick Hopfensperger, Curriculum Writer

Sunil Koswatta, Mathematician, Grade 8

Brian Kotz, Curriculum Writer

Henry Kranendonk, Statistics Lead Curriculum Writer / Editor

Connie Laughlin, Math Auditor

Jennifer Loftin, Program Manager – Professional Development

Abby Mattern, Math Auditor

Nell McAnelly, Project Director

Saki Milton, Curriculum Writer

Pia Mohsen, Curriculum Writer

Jerry Moreno, Statistician

Ann Netter, Lead Curriculum Writer / Editor, Grades 6-7

Roxy Peck, Statistician, Statistics Lead Curriculum Writer / Editor

Terrie Poehl, Math Auditor

Spencer Roby, Math Auditor

Kathleen Scholand, Math Auditor

Erika Silva, Lead Curriculum Writer / Editor, Grade 6-7

Hester Sutton, Advisor / Reviewer Grades 6-7

Shannon Vinson, Statistics Lead Curriculum Writer / Editor

Julie Wortmann, Lead Curriculum Writer / Editor, Grade 7

David Wright, Mathematician, Lead Curriculum Writer / Editor, Grades 6-7

Kristen Zimmerman, Document Production Manager